WORD
OF
KNOWLEDGE

A Charismatic Gift

Rev. Robert DeGrandis, SSJ

With Mrs. Jessie Borrello

Published by:
**Praising God Catholic Association
of Texas.**

CONTENTS

Chapter One

TWO PRINCIPLES OF HEALING

*". . .when anything is exposed by the light, it be-
comes visible, for anything that becomes visible is
light. Therefore it is said, Awake, O sleeper, and
arise from the dead, and Christ shall give you light."
(Eph 5:13-14)*

The common charismatic revelational gifts are word of wisdom, word of knowledge and discernment (cf 1 Cor 12:8-11).
Frequently, while using these gifts, especially word of knowledge, there are two principles of healing which interact. A clearer
understanding of these two principles will enable one to more
adequately communicate healing prayer in the power of the Holy
Spirit.

The *first principle*: Our whole emotional life begins not
just with our conscious mind, but in the depths of our being,
below the level of consciousness, in the unconscious.

The *second principle*: We do not treat symptoms when
praying with someone for healing, but we search and pray

through root causes of hurt, injury and trauma which, in many cases, are repressed in the unconscious.

Through the charismatic revelational gift of word of knowledge, we are enabled to go to the very depths of a person's being. The Holy Spirit reveals, or gives insight to us as we are praying with another for inner healing. Thus we can "see" or "perceive" with the inner eyes of the Spirit what is buried in a person's unconscious.

As we pray with a person for the healing of a negative repressed emotion or trauma, our purpose and goal is to expose that trauma to the healing light of Jesus. The presence of Jesus is healing and in many instances, the person being prayed for can be healed of physical, emotional or spiritual symptoms. This is inner healing, which is healing of the inner person. Inner healing is far-reaching in that it has outward physical, psychological, spiritual and relational effects.

Ruth Carter Stapleton states in the introduction of her book *The Gift of Inner Healing:*

> When we speak of inner healing, we refer to the experience in which the Holy Spirit restores health to the deepest area of our lives by dealing with the root cause of our hurts and pain.[1]

First Principle — Conscious and Unconscious Mind

Our conscious mind, what we are aware of, accounts for only 10% of our total consciousness. The unconscious accounts

[1] Ruth Carter Stapleton, *The Gift of Inner Healing* (Waco, Texas: Word, Incorporated, 1976), Introduction.

for the remaining 90%. This seems a little lopsided, doesn't it, considering how "awareness" oriented we are in our modern Western world. However, it is generally agreed in the field of psychology that our consciousness accounts for only 10%. The remaining 90% is in the unconscious.

Many times the image of an iceberg is used to illustrate the distinction between the two. The tip of the iceberg above the surface represents the conscious part of ourselves. The rest of the iceberg, massively submerged below in the depths, is likened to the unconscious.

Because of this, we could say that our whole emotional life, along with all of our life's energies, begins in the unconscious. Our unconscious mind from the moment of conception has faithfully recorded every experience, event, memory and emotion for us. It is a faithful computer. This is our "personal unconscious". Therefore, our emotional life, which is rooted in the unconscious, reverts back to our mother's womb, to earliest childhood, to youth, adolescence, up to the present time. Nothing is left unrecorded—forgotten, yes—but still affecting us.

Why is this principle important to the healing ministry? Because in the healing ministry we need to remember we are contending with these two levels of a person—conscious and unconscious. What a person might think (conscious) to be his or her problem might not be the problem at all. In most cases, negative repressed emotional trauma, hurt or unresolved conflict in a person's past is negatively affecting present circumstances.

For instance, a person's anxiety with a spouse might not really be a marital problem, but could be a repressed feeling of hurt and anger going back to a parent's lack of affection or attention which could have happened at the age of two. A present problem can and usually does trigger off a similar repressed trauma dating back to earliest childhood. Even though a person is not aware of this consciously, the memory of the trauma is still recorded.

So in most cases we are really dealing with unconscious

material. We, as ministers of healing, would have no prior knowledge of these hidden traumas. As we pray, seeking help from the Holy Spirit through the common charismatic gifts, it is the Holy spirit that will reveal, especially through word of knowledge, what the real root cause or causes of a person's problems are. Then we proceed with wisdom as the Holy Spirit directs. We move in his power.

The charismatic gift of word of knowledge is the diagnosis of the Holy Spirit.

The charismatic gift of word of wisdom is the prescription of the Holy Spirit.

Some would say that those definitions are too simplistic; however, in my mind, it helps to clarify the distinction between these two charismatic/revelational gifts.

So within the depths of the human mind lie all the events and memories of the past filed away faithfully. Feelings and behavioral responses are also recorded.

Agnes Sanford in her book *The Healing Gifts of the Spirit* cites the following example from her own life. This story should help us to understand how memories and feelings are buried within us. Also it is an example of how a word of knowledge, given to Agnes Sanford by a friend, helped her to identify a repressed fear which was rooted in her childhood.

A discerning young woman once said to me, "As I was praying it came to me that there is a fear in you which is connected with the eighth year of your life."

This struck me as authentic. If she had said, "God told me you were to go and see so-and-so and pray for her," I am afraid I would have suspected a slight unconscious tendency to influence my will by her will.

But I tested the guidance, hearkened to the words of my friend and said, "What is it, Lord?"

Then I sent my mind back in time and tried to remember the eighth year of my life and to review it, so that God through the subconscious mind could put His finger on a sore spot and say, "That is it." It was a year full of happy memories — white violets, lace-leaved, blooming in dark loam; mountaintops red and purple with wild azaleas; the Big Stream foaming down the valley overhung with a more fragrant foam of blossoming shrubs all growing wild in a wonderland of beauty. Yet, as I searched, I remembered among these lovely pictures another picture that was filled with fear: I saw myself standing at the window, nose to pane, watching for my father and mother to come home from their afternoon walk and being literally sick with terror. I remembered also that never in my life had I spoken of this fear to anyone. And God brought me to see, what I had never seen before, that I had hidden the cause of the fear even from myself. For the first time, following the hint given by a friend, I realized that I had feared that my father would die.

Now of what use could this be, this remembering of the cause? Would it relieve my fear merely to understand it and say to myself, "So I must learn to live with it"?

I do not think so. "But I don't want to learn to live with it!" my rebellious soul shouted within me, knowing that there is a better way than this. I went back in the memories and found that little child, and playing a game in the imagination, I told her that she was loved and comforted and that she would also be healed. Opening thus a door into the past, I took Jesus with me and led Him to her that He might heal her with His love. And being of a sacramental church, I went to Communion service the next Sunday taking her with me.

When I turned back and found that little child in me and took her to Jesus in the way that was most natural to me, then the door was opened so that Jesus Christ entered into that living memory and healed it just as though He had walked back through time and found the little girl and had taken the fear away from her by restoring to her a father whole and joyous and able to show his love. I do not say that this was completely or instantaneously done, but I do say that perceiving the beginning of a certain fear and believing that Jesus Christ could take that fear away began a healing.[2]

I highly recommend all of Agnes Sanford's books. Her insights are of great value to us in the healing ministry.

Also Robert Faricy, S.J., in his book *Praying for Inner Healing* helps us to understand a little further this first principle:

Where do these—mostly unconscious—hurts come from? They come from the very beginning of our existence, from our earliest years, from our childhood and growing up, from the whole process of living. Some of them are so early and so deeply repressed that we can never get at them; but Our Lord sees them all and can heal them all. Many interior wounds, both

---

[2] Agnes Sanford, *Healing Gifts of the Spirit* (Philadelphia and New York: Trumpet Books, A.J. Holman Company, division of J.B. Lippincott Company, 1966), pp. 102-3.

conscious and buried, result from poor or inadequate home life in childhood, from negative aspects of school life, from setbacks in childhood or in later life. In many cases, things have been done to people which ought never to have been done, a lot of suffering was caused, and healing is needed.[3]

Another example: Perhaps we are afraid of the dark, or water, or of loud noises, such as the sirens on fire engines, police cars, or the loud noise of a train. These present feelings of fear are unexplainable, yet they are very real to us. When we are experiencing fear of the dark and we cannot consciously connect this fear with any event in our conscious memory, then we can be fairly certain that this fear is emerging from the depths of our unconscious.

The present fear we are experiencing is a behavioral response which is rooted in a past trauma. Perhaps we were left in the dark as a child which created an unconscious fear of the dark. Our unconscious mind with its good and bad memories has stored away that trauma which could affect our present behavior.

When someone is praying with us, word of knowledge is of the utmost importance because it helps us to pinpoint root causes. It is the work of the Holy Spirit to manifest himself through us in this way. It is the Spirit's work to reveal troublesome areas for the Lord Jesus wants us joyous and free. As the negative trauma is released and healed, we are able to receive the Lord's love more abundantly. By sorting out and identifying these areas of emotional turmoil, we will remove some of the barriers we have to receiving the Lord's love. The negative walls of the past tumble down. We experience the Lord's love in a new way, a deeper and fuller way.

[3] Robert Faricy, S.J., *Praying for Inner Healing* (New York/Ramsey: Paulist Press, 1979), p. 8.

Fr. Robert Faricy gives us an example of how we may pray for personal inner healing.

> In prayer, I can take the Lord's hand and let him walk back in time, in my own personal history, to the time and place where I was hurt. I can ask him to be present in that hurtful situation — in the home, or in the classroom, or on the playground — filling it with his healing love. And I can ask him to take the pain out of the memory, to remove all fear and anxiety and guilt and anger associated with that memory, and to fill the places where they were with his love, healing the memory. I pray not that the memory disappear, but that its meaning be changed so that I can praise God and even thank him for what happened, knowing that he writes straight with crooked lines and that the healed memory will mean the conversion of past hurts into greater understanding of the hurts of others, into a broader and deeper compassion or in some other positive force.[4]

In inner healing, as in all types of healing, THE PRESENCE OF JESUS BRINGS HEALING TO ANY SITUATION. We bring everything to him who heals, touches and makes us whole.

As we expose more and more of ourselves to the healing light of Jesus, the burdens and negativity we carry will begin to dissipate. As the light of Jesus Christ enters, we can more fully echo what St. Paul wrote to the Ephesians:

> . . . *and to know the love of Christ which*
> *surpasses knowledge, that you may be filled*
> *with all the fulness of God.* (Eph 3:17-19)

[4]Ibid, pp. 9-10.

I also want to mention briefly that introducing the possibility of forgiveness is a safeguard in any healing situation. We ask forgiveness for and from the persons or person involved in the trauma since forgiveness does bring us more fully into the healing love of Jesus. In my book, *To Forgive Is Divine*, I cover this subject of forgiveness.[5]

Inner healing prayer many times brings instantaneous healing for physical, psychological or spiritual problems. Perhaps for others "soaking" prayer might be needed as there are many layers to our being. What we might touch upon at one occasion of healing prayer might need to be touched upon at a deeper level in a subsequent session. "Soaking" prayer is repeated prayer focused upon one area of a person's life or upon a particular physical, psychological and spiritual situation that needs healing. We "soak" the event with prayer. Francis MacNutt in his book, *The Power to Heal*, deals exclusively with soaking prayer. He gives us these practical examples:

> This means that soaking prayer can be something we do at regular intervals; parents can pray for five minutes a day for their retarded child; or we can try praying once a week for 15 minutes with an arthritic friend. On the other hand, we can decide to take a long time in one chunk and make an all-out effort; for example, a small group may decide to spend a whole afternoon, or a whole day, praying for a friend who has multiple sclerosis.
>
> If we are going to spend considerable time with a person, we should ordinarily have some indication—

[5] Robert DeGrandis, S.S.J., *To Forgive Is Divine* (HOM Books, 108 Aberdeen Street, Lowell, MA 01850).

through gift of knowledge or some other sign — that we should spend that much time.[6]

Use the following points as a guideline in a healing prayer session or for your own inner healing prayer during personal prayer time.

1. Pray in tongues softly.
2. Ask the Holy Spirit to reveal root causes of some negative memory/trauma of our lives especially from conception through adolescence.
3. Invite Jesus' presence into any past traumatic situation, event or emotion as revealed by the Holy Spirit through word of knowledge.
4. Ask the Lord for healing of root causes.
5. Ask forgiveness and extend forgiveness to all involved, including ourselves.
6. Ask the Lord's forgiveness for the ways in which we have harbored unforgiveness and resentment, also for the ways in which we have allowed the effects of any negativity to influence our lives to date.
7. Give thanks and praise.

Blessing and glory and wisdom and
thanksgiving and honor and power and might
be to our God for ever and ever! Amen. (Rev 7:12)

Jesus Christ is the same
yesterday, today and forever. (Heb 13:8)

This scripture is important for us to remember when we pray for inner healing. We can ask Jesus to walk back in time to

[6] Francis MacNutt, *The Power to Heal* (Notre Dame, Indiana: Ave Maria Press, 1977), p. 42.

heal the memory of any traumatic event in our lives. He is eternally present to us—whether it was a time many years ago or as recent as yesterday—Jesus is there.

Remember we stated earlier that the common charismatic gifts are a sign of Jesus' power and presence among us. Without the charismatic/revelational gifts of the Holy Spirit we would only be operating on a conscious level. With the charismatic gifts we can function within the depths of a person's unconscious to bring about more lasting healing.

Second Principle—Root Causes

The second principle actually has been touched upon already in the first principle. If we recall, it is this: we do not treat symptoms when praying with a person for healing, but we search for root causes.

To illustrate this principle, let the image of crabgrass come into your mind. If you pull crabgrass at the ground level, it will grow up again because the root is still below the surface. We can make this analogy to healing when people sometimes say, "I've lost my healing. I was healed, but I am not healed anymore." I do not believe you ever lose a healing. What I believe is that the root cause of the problem still exists in the unconscious. These people were only partially healed as the area below the level of consciousness was not touched upon and the root causes were not exposed and brought to Jesus for healing. If root causes remain, our emotional/physical/spiritual turmoil will "grow" again, just as crabgrass only snipped reappears.

A woman once wrote to me this statement concerning her healing: "Word of knowledge touched me deeply. I personally was healed of a situation in my life that I'd been praying about for years." Word of knowledge can bring about lasting healing!

Fr. Emilien Tardif states in his book, *Jesus Is Alive:*

One day an afflicted woman came to see me with her daughter who, due to a strange illness, had to abandon her studies. They told me the young girl suffered from strange attacks. She would frequently faint and have convulsions similar to those of epilepsy. They had gone to several doctors with negative results. They consulted psychologists and did not see any improvement. They even had the stupidity to consult witches. They finally reached the conclusion that she needed an exorcism.

The mother talked and the young girl remained silent. She did not even answer my questions. Since I did not have any information, and not knowing what to pray for, I prayed in tongues. Suddenly a word constantly repeated itself in my mind: abortion. I opened my eyes and asked her if she had anything to do with abortion. She was surprised and asked me: "Who told you?"

With tears in her eyes, she told me she had had extramarital relations with her boyfriend, and had become pregnant. Since she belonged to a very well-known family, she was afraid, and decided to have an abortion. She then had to carry the double weight of her sin, the thought of which made her faint.

She repented and confessed, and we prayed for her inner healing. The Lord forgave and healed her, and she never fainted again. The Lord had given us knowledge of the root of the problem. She was not possessed and had no physical problem.[7]

[7] Emilien Tardif, *Jesus Is Alive* (Montreal QC H2W 1R3: Editions INTER, 1985), pp. 55-6.

The charismatic/revelational gifts of the Holy Spirit will lead us into the depths of a person and into our own depths. It is here that lasting healing can be effected. It is to the root causes that we direct our prayer and it is to these roots that the Holy Spirit will lead us. Then we are not snipping the crabgrass on the surface, but we are digging deeply and getting all the roots out so the crabgrass will appear no more.

Also because of the principle of the 90% unconscious mind, we can never say to others, "You were not healed because of lack of faith." That statement is too simplistic and does not take into account the principle of the unconscious mind and root causes of a person's illness.

In speaking to a person about faith, you have to distinguish between faith on a conscious level and faith on an unconscious level. What is the difference between the two? Most people have faith on a conscious level and it is injurious to say to them, "You don't have faith," because on a conscious level they are saying, "Lord, I believe." Maybe on an unconscious level faith is lacking and that is where we can appeal to the Lord saying, "Lord, help my unbelief." This is a very delicate area in the healing ministry and one in which much harm is done. The person who is being prayed with might feel guilty if his or her inner faith is questioned. Most people don't know the depths of their own being as the Spirit does and their ability to be healed has nothing to do with their lack of faith. An openness to using the gifts of the Holy Spirit to reveal root causes can often get to the bottom of a person's physical, psychological or spiritual disorder. Their openness and desire to be healed attest to their faith.

Many times people will have trouble relating to Jesus Christ on a deep faith level because they have never had a good father relationship. They have never had a deep experience or relationship with a man, and Jesus is a man. Therefore, one does not need to be pressed into questioning one's faith on a conscious level; one does need to be healed of the imperfect relationship they have had with men in general and in particular with their own father.

From one viewpoint healing is simple, "Ask, and it will be given to you; search, and you will find; knock, and the door will be opened to you. For the one who asks always receives; the one who searches always finds; the one who knocks will always have the door opened to him" (Mt 7:7).

From another viewpoint healing is complex because we are complex. We are dealing with the complexity of the human mind and personality. This is why we need the Holy Spirit's power to help us.

Lord, you have examined me and you know me. You know everything I do; from far away you understand all my thoughts.

Psalm 139:1-2

To summarize this chapter:

** Our conscious mind accounts for 10% of our being. We use as an example the tip, the surface, of an iceberg.

** Our unconscious mind accounts for the remaining 90%. The example is the remainder of the iceberg, which is submerged below the surface.

** Our unconscious mind has faithfully recorded every experience, event and memory for us.

** In the healing ministry we need to remember we are contending with these two levels as we pray — the conscious and the unconscious.

** The Holy Spirit reveals root causes of a person's problems through word of knowledge. As we ask, we shall receive.

** We would otherwise have no knowledge of a person's repressed emotions or traumas.

** Word of knowledge is the diagnosis. We ask the Lord, "What is it?"

** Word of wisdom is the prescription. "What do we do, Lord?"

** The presence of Jesus can bring healing in any situation.

** We invite Jesus into the negative situation, trauma, emotion for lasting healing on a deep-root level.

** The possibility of forgiveness should be expressed in all healing situations.

** Continuing, ongoing, "soaking" prayer might be needed on occasions as there are many layers to our being.

** Jesus Christ is the same yesterday, today and tomorrow.

** With the charismatic gifts of the Holy Spirit we are operating, not only on a conscious level, but into the depths of a person's unconscious.

** Root causes are like crabgrass. If we just pull up crabgrass at the ground level, it will continue to grow. We need to dig deeply and pull out the roots.

** There are two levels of faith — conscious faith and unconscious faith.

** Healing is simple because the Lord tells us to "ask to receive."

** Healing is complex because we are complex.

** Always give thanks to the Lord.

*So if the Son makes you free,
you will be free indeed.* (Jn 8:36)

Chapter Two

UNDERSTANDING WORD OF KNOWLEDGE

*. . .to another the word of knowledge
by the same Spirit . . .* (1 Cor 12:8)

*People must think of us as Christ's servants,
stewards entrusted with the mysteries of God.
What is expected of stewards is that each one
should be found worthy of his trust.* (1 Cor 4:1-2)

Word of knowledge is a word or fact given to us by the Holy Spirit by which we gain information necessary to heal and renew members of the Body of Christ.

People in prayer groups all over the world are experiencing the charismatic gift of word of knowledge. Many times they do not recognize this as a manifestation or movement of the Holy Spirit and their internal questioning goes something like this:

• What is "this thought, word, picture, or insight" that seems to come into my mind as I pray with people?

- How did I receive that insight or knowledge into this person's life?
- Where did "this thought, word, picture, insight, perception or intuition" originate?
- How did I know that which was previously unknown to me?

The thought that this might be word of knowledge comes from one's reading on the subject of charismatic gifts, but then many are still not sure since written material is limited on this particular charismatic gift. As with many unanswered questions, we continue to search for answers through books or we seek out others with some experience in this field and learn from them. In this chapter I share my experiences and thoughts concerning word of knowledge in response to such requests being made of me.

Several years ago a young woman asked me to pray with her for unexplained anxiety. As we were praying, the Holy Spirit revealed to me, through the word of knowledge, that there was a death in her family when she was three years old. I asked her, "Did someone die in your family when you were three?" She said, "I don't remember. If someone did, I cannot recall." As we were finishing our prayer session, I asked her, "If you ever find this to be true, would you let me know?" She agreed.

Some time later, she went to her mother and asked her if this were true. Her mother replied, "Yes, it is. Your grandfather died when you were that age. You were very close to him and loved him very much. He was in a rest home when he died. While he was there his appearance changed a lot. Later when you saw him at the funeral parlor you were shocked. He didn't look like the grandfather you once knew and cared for so much. One of the changes was that all of his hair had been cut off. You didn't recognize him and you were afraid."

Her mother had confirmed the word of knowledge. In a subsequent healing prayer session we prayed, asking Jesus to be present with her during that time in her life. We asked Jesus to set her free from the negative influences of this childhood memory. Jesus did heal the negative memories. Through prayer, she was set free, and was released from her unexplained anxiety.

This story brings us to highlight many points concerning word of knowledge:

1. *She was experiencing unexplained anxiety.*

Repressed anxiety and fear over her grandfather's death was buried in the unconscious. It is an accepted fact that these types of repressed emotions control our lives more than we realize.

Agnes Sanford, in one of her classic books, *The Healing Gifts of the Spirit*, states it this way:

> Something is troubling the deep mind. There is no question about it. Some old unpleasant memory is knocking at the doors of the consciousness. Some need of the soul is rising as a dark shadow that will overwhelm us if we do not let it out into the light of understanding. We do indeed need more of the Holy Spirit at such times as these, but the gift we need is the gift of knowledge, particularly the knowledge and understanding of our own souls. And it is the primary work of the Holy Spirit to give us this understanding if we will but ask and listen to His answer.[8]

2. Concerning this woman's anxiety, *I asked the Spirit to reveal a word of knowledge to me.*

Word of knowledge is manifested through us in many ways, but for the purpose it serves in this example, we could define it as one of the nine common charismatic gifts of the Spirit whereby the Lord imparts or reveals to us a word or a fact which was previously unknown. It is a manifestation of the knowledge of the Lord about a particular situation. That word will ulti-

---

[8] Sanford, *Healing Gifts of the Spirit,* p. 94.

mately bear good fruit and will lead us to praise and worship the Lord Jesus.

Many times we see this gift manifested through a vision, through a word flashed on the screen of one's mind, through an intuitive sense or through an emotion concerning an area in a person's life that needs healing.

3. The *"word" I heard in my mind was "death."*

This is the way in which word of knowledge is usually manifested through me. It is through a "word" that I hear in my mind. Additionally another "word" was given which gave specific age — third year. This is not unusual and happens frequently in the healing ministry.

Emilien Tardif in his book, *Jesus Is Alive*, also writes this of his personal experience with word of knowledge:

> A clear idea comes to mind. As we communicate it, additional details are revealed to us. I would compare this experience to reading a message written on tissues pulled from a kleenex box. On the first tissue there are some words I have to read. I then pull out that kleenex, take another one, and read what the second one says. What is written on the third cannot be read or understood if the other two have not been pulled out. In the same manner, as one starts communicating the first message, it is immediately completed as it is being transmitted.[9]

Word of knowledge comes as a thought, a vision, a word, a sense or by an emotion. With time, encouragement and continued use of the word of knowledge, you will develop and come to recognize the way in which this charismatic gift will be manifested through you.

---

[9] Tardif, Jesus is Alive, p. 58.

4. *She did not remember.*

Frequently, a word of knowledge is denied because the person being prayed over is not consciously aware of the event that the Holy Spirit is revealing. We have to be willing to bring it to his light and love for healing to take place.

Later, especially when praying for healing of memories in a follow-up session, the person will usually confirm the word of knowledge. This often happens as consciousness has time to accept it. It is brought out of darkness into light. In this case, however, someone in her family confirmed what she was too young to remember.

5. *It is the Lord's love that heals in any situation.*

As we prayerfully sought the Lord for the root cause of this young woman's anxiety, the problem was revealed and the Lord's light was focused like a laser beam on the anxiety.

Today, the same as it was 2000 years ago, it is Jesus' love that heals. "Jesus Christ is the same today as he was yesterday and as he will be for ever" (Heb 13:8). Jesus heals today.

6. *She was released from her unexplained anxiety.* When I met with the young woman in a follow-up healing session, our prayer was focused upon bringing the Lord's light and love back into the traumatic event.

Also, during this time, she expressed a loving act, an act of forgiveness, to those who were involved. She needed to forgive those who brought her unprepared into the funeral parlor. She also needed to forgive her grandfather for dying. Even though consciously no one intended any harm and surely not her grandfather, to the mind of a three-year-old it was indeed damaging. As youngsters, we live mostly by feelings. So, with a conscious act of the will of her adult mind, and with her imagination, we brought the three-year-old child to Jesus for healing.

As Agnes Sanford states:

How can he come into that memory and change it? I

do not know. It is the greatest of all mysteries. But I know that he can do so.[10]

Our need to understand, in most instances, is universal. In the spiritual realm, it is also natural that we desire to understand the workings of the Lord in our lives. In other words, "What are you doing, Lord? What's really going on here?" Most of the time the understanding we seek comes after we have placed our faith and trust in him.

In all ways and in all things we need to:

Trust in the Lord with all your heart;
and do not rely on your own insight.
In all your ways acknowledge him,
and he will make straight your paths. (Prv 3:5-6)

As we grasp what the Lord has done and is doing, our appreciation of his love for us deepens. This appreciation and awareness lead us into deeper praise for the wonders he has performed and is performing.

O give thanks to the Lord, for he is good,
for his steadfast love endures for ever. (Ps 136:1)

Understanding word of knowledge and seeing it manifested leads one to increased praise. Through word of knowledge I have seen miracle upon miracle performed as the Lord has set his people free of spiritual, emotional, physical and psychological bondages. I join with those who have been set free in such a way to say, "Thank you, Lord, for your signs and wonders manifested through us. With grateful hearts, we say, 'Thank you.' "

The following is a testimony I received from a woman who

[10] Sanford, *Healing Gifts of the Spirit,* p. 104.

shared with me the signs, wonders and power of the Lord in her life:

There wasn't a part of me that did not hurt physically, mentally or spiritually. So much had happened to me, especially in the past few years, that I got to a point where I couldn't think clearly.

About five years ago I came very close to committing suicide. At a healing service you called out that someone was being healed of the memory of an attempted suicide. I just couldn't own up to it but I was the one who received a healing of that memory.

At my last visit to the doctor, my checkup showed that my heart and lungs were healed and my pressure has returned to normal. My medication has been reduced. Next week I will be taken off all medication.

Today I feel like a new creation!

It is as if I were never sick. I feel, for the first time in many years, alive and well. Every day is a fresh start with an added promise. I have come to enjoy the gift of myself. It is as if life has just begun. I am able to laugh and smile for the first time in years.

Thank you, Jesus.

Jesus came to "heal the brokenhearted." What he has done for one, he can do for all.

As the charismatic gifts of the Holy Spirit became more commonly exercised, one by one, each was spectacular. The gift of speaking in tongues, the gift of prophecy, the gift of healing and miracles come to my mind as being the spectacular gifts of the '70s. Could we not say that word of wisdom, word of knowledge and discernment are the gifts that God wishes his people to use more effectively at this time? I believe they are. We must remember, however, that we do not look to the gift itself or to the one through whom the charismatic gift operates. Instead we look to Jesus and to the fruit the gift bears in our lives. The charismatic gifts are not meant to be spectacular in and for themselves. They are meant to show the power and presence of the Lord Jesus.

For where two or three meet in my name,
I shall be there with them. (Mt 18:20)

Charismatic gifts are signs of the presence and power of Jesus as we gather together in his name. Many times a charismatic gift, particularly word of knowledge, comes on the firing line precisely because, as the first example of the young woman I prayed with illustrates, we are entering into the depths of a person's life. We are unlocking negative secrets of the past which often require deep forgiveness. They are often hard to face. However, it is my experience and it is the experience of many, that as we allow the Lord to heal us of these negative repressed areas, then the space in our soul which was previously occupied with this repressed material can now be filled with his love, so to speak. The Lord wants to fill us with his love — more than we could ever hope or imagine. It is his purpose for us to be one with him and to be filled with his love.

As you read on it is my wish that you will be open to the ways that the Lord wishes to heal you. I join with St. Paul in praying this prayer for you:

Out of his infinite glory, may he give you
the power through his Spirit for your hidden
self to grow strong, so that Christ may live

in your hearts through faith, and then,
planted in love and built on love, you will
with all the saints have strength to grasp the
breadth and the length, the height and
the depth, until, knowing the love of Christ,
which is beyond all knowledge you are filled
with the utter fullness of God.
(Eph 3:16-19)

My First Experience

During an interview recently, someone asked me if I could remember the first time I had experienced word of knowledge. That experience was in August of 1970. I had been in the Catholic Charismatic Renewal less than a year. I was praying with a woman when I suddenly saw a whiskey bottle in my mind. I pushed the thought out. It came back. I pushed it out again. It came back again. Three times this happened. So finally I asked her, "What does a whiskey bottle mean to you?" She said, "Well, when I go home to visit my father, who is an alcoholic, I tend to overdrink with him. I feel guilty because sometimes I get drunk. All I really want to do is to spend time visiting with him."

Afterwards we were able to focus our prayer on her guilty feelings. She also forgave both herself and her father for overdrinking. Additionally, we prayed about her relationship with her father. We asked the Lord to set her free so she would be able to visit with him without drinking excessively.

I tell of my own first experience to illustrate that most people who are moving in the charismatic gift of word of knowledge do not even realize it. I was and didn't realize it the first time.

It is a valid principle that when you are baptized in the Holy Spirit you begin to move in the Holy Spirit much more than you realize. I've found that to be true in the twenty-two countries in which I have worked.

Father Emilien Tardif tells us of his first example of word of knowledge:

> I went on horseback to visit a community hidden in the mountains. I celebrated Mass and prayed for the sick. While I prayed in tongues, a word repeatedly came into my mind very strongly: epilepsy. I went on praying, then remained silent, and finally I took a risk in faith and asked, "Is there someone here with epilepsy? The Lord is healing him now."
>
> There were moments of tense silence that seemed to me to last forever, until the school principal raised her hand and said, "Father, it is my daughter. Look at her." Next to her, a young girl around fifteen years of age was trembling and perspiring. She had been ill since birth, but the Lord healed her completely and she has never since had another attack.
>
> This was the first time I received the charismatic gift of knowledge.[11]

Jesus' Experience With Word of Knowledge

When Jesus met the Samaritan woman at the well (John 4), he was moved by the Spirit to reveal her whole life to her. After her encounter with Jesus, she said this to the townspeople, "Come and see a man who has told me everything I ever did . . ." (Jn 4:30).

[11] Tardif, *Jesus Is Alive*, pp. 56-7.

Jesus had revealed her whole life. How? For her to have made such an all-encompassing statement to the townspeople where she lived, she must have spoken with Jesus for some time. In the beginning of their conversation Jesus revealed his knowledge of her five husbands, but later she said that "everything" she ever did was revealed. I believe that Jesus manifested a series of words of knowledge concerning her past life.

It is much like the statement quoted earlier by Father Emilien Tardif, that when one word of knowledge is used, another follows, like tissues being pulled out of a box. Among other lessons, this scripture story is a lesson in Jesus' use of word of knowledge.

Earlier I explained how word of knowledge could be used to bring hidden traumas and repressed negative emotions out of darkness to the light of Christ for healing. In the Samaritan woman's story, the Lord revealed brokenness in her life. God's love and grace is always there but sometimes it is the unresolved brokenness in us which blocks the Lord's love from entering more fully.

Let us now turn to Jesus' experience.

When Jesus asked her for water from the well, he said to her:

> *Whoever drinks this water will get thirsty*
> *again; but anyone who drinks the water that I*
> *shall give will never be thirsty again: the water*
> *that I shall give will turn into a spring inside*
> *him, welling up to eternal life.* (Jn 4:13-14)

We experience this living water of the Spirit especially during Mass, prayer meetings and healing services. The Holy Spirit comes alive within us.

> *"Sir," said the woman, "give me some of that*
> *water, so that I may never get thirsty and never*

have to come here again to draw water." "Go
and call your husband," said Jesus to her, "and
come back here." The woman answered, "I have
no husband." He said to her, "You are right to
say, 'I have no husband'; for although you
have had five, the one you have now is not your
husband. You spoke the truth there." (Jn 4:15-19)

It was supernaturally revealed to Jesus that this woman had
five husbands. Later, because of this interchange:

Many Samaritans of that town had believed in
him on the strength of the woman's testimony
when she said, "He told me all I have ever done." (Jn 4:39-40)

He stayed for two days, and when he spoke to
them many more came to believe; and they said
to the woman, "Now, we no longer believe because of what you
told us; we have heard him
ourselves and we know that he really is
the savior of the world." (Jn 4:41-42)

As we did before with my personal experience story, let us
look at this story in Jesus' everyday life. We will again see certain principles which reveal to us the process, value and effect
of the gift of word of knowledge.

1. PROCESS: *Jesus was open to the movement of the Holy*
Spirit.

These "words" were supernaturally revealed and were not
known through natural means or natural knowledge. It was su-
pernatural knowledge given by the Holy Spirit. As we follow in
the footsteps of Jesus' example, it is always better that we seek
to yield to the movement of the Holy Spirit. In that way we are
operating according to his manner, not ours. The yielding is our

action; the work is his. Using word of knowledge is a yielding to the manner of the Holy Spirit.

2. PROCESS: *Jesus knew in his mind "five husbands."*

Also the Samaritan woman said, "He told me all I have ever done" (Jn 4:40). We can only guess as to what else Jesus revealed to her. We do know he told her "all," or some Bible translations state "everything." How did this knowledge come to Jesus? One of the ways in which word of knowledge comes is through a word "heard" or "seen." There is a "knowing" because it has been "seen" or "heard" on the screen of one's mind, an inner vision. Jesus experienced this inner knowing.

3. VALUE: The word of knowledge that Jesus manifested was *part of ordinary living.*

Jesus was tired by the journey into Samaria when he met the woman at the well. I want to stress using word of knowledge as part of everyday life. In the following section I will explain how word of knowledge is valuable for us every day.

4. VALUE: *Jesus revealed unresolved brokenness in her life* through word of knowledge.

Word of knowledge will lead one to areas needing repentance and forgiveness. It directs attention to that which needs the healing power of Jesus.

As repressed hurts surface one may need to ask forgiveness from the Lord for the ways in which they have allowed unconfessed past hurts to fester through unforgiveness. In other words, one can give darkness a home through unforgiveness. Extending forgiveness to another or to ourselves creates a special place within us for the Lord's love to abide.

5. EFFECT: *Jesus' presence brought healing to the woman's life.*

We do not know anything of this woman before she came into contact with Jesus except that she had five husbands. After her encounter with Jesus we know she believed and became a witness for Jesus. She experienced healing on a deep personal level. Scripture tells us that she shared her belief and many came to believe on the strength of her personal testimony. I am sure you have seen this occurrence. As Jesus' presence and love enter and touch a person's life, they frequently share their testimonies of healing. Their faith is contagious!

The charismatic gift of word of knowledge, when it is manifested, does have a kind of "rippling effect" of increased faith and healing upon a community.

6. EFFECT: *The fruit that this "word" or "words" bore was the belief of the whole town in Jesus as the Savior of the world.*

Word of knowledge will bring many to deep or deeper faith.

In Father Emilien Tardif's book, *Jesus Is Alive*, he states this:

> How can we recognize the authenticity of a word of knowledge? Only by the results. The testimonies are the thermometer which determines if the word truly came from the Lord or not. Certain ministries will not produce fruit if they are not accompanied by testimonies. For example, if a healing is announced by a word of knowledge, but it is not authenticated with testimonies, it would result in something doubtful, and would also give rise to criticism instead of praise to the Lord.[12]

One of the fruits that word of knowledge bears is the testimony of the person healed. What do we look for in a person's testimony?

For healing
For deeper faith
For renewed life
For joy

[12] Emilien Tardif, *Jesus Is Alive*, p. 58.

For an outpouring of the Father's love

For power and strength beyond a person's capabilities

To proclaiming Jesus as Lord

To praising God

Yes, all of these and more will be evidenced, to some degree, when it is an authentic movement of the Holy Spirit.

The same Holy Spirit that led Jesus to speak to the Samaritan woman 2000 years ago is still working through us and with us today — revealing, leading, directing, empowering — if we but yield and step out in faith.

To condense Jesus' experience with word of knowledge with the woman at the well:

PROCESS: Jesus was open to the movement of the Holy Spirit.

PROCESS: Jesus knew in his mind "five husbands."

VALUE: Jesus revealed her brokenness through word of knowledge.

EFFECT: Jesus' presence brought healing to her.

EFFECT: Deep or deeper faith in Jesus was felt throughout the whole community.

Healing Services

In my own healing ministry one of the clearest examples of word of knowledge operating through me is during healing services. I pray a simple prayer, "Lord, touch and heal your people," and "word" of knowledge begins to flow. I believe that as I ask, I shall receive (Mt 7:7). Words such as "hearts," "backs," "ears," "marriages" start to come to me. Then I know that backs are being healed, hearts are being repaired, ears are being opened, marriages are being mended. The Lord is revealing what he is doing among his people. He is revealing what healings are taking place in the group. I always ask people to hold up their hands if they are healed. Through the testimony of these people being healed we know that the Lord's power is breaking through.

The following are testimonies I have received over the years. I thank the Lord for each and every healing.

> As you were calling out healings for arthritis, you said someone was being healed in the neck joint. I have had a lot of pain for a number of years in this joint. It was getting progressively worse. The pain was unbearable. It left me unable to get proper sleep which caused me to be in a cranky mood most of the time.
>
> When you called out that someone was being healed of this problem, I raised my hand.
>
> Praise God! I have been healed. I have not had one bit of pain since then.
>
> All praise and glory to Jesus!

Another woman's testimony:

> I raised my hand and felt extreme heat being applied all over my back. It felt like it was on fire. I even felt like something was being "knit" together down there.
>
> When I got home that night I thought I would try to touch my toes. I tried. I did it — without pain — for the first time in months!
>
> Glory be to Jesus!

A man's testimony from another country:

> This is to witness to a healing I received at a rally

recently. The healing was for a severe heart condition from which I have been suffering for the past twenty years.

My first heart attack left my heart permanently damaged with "bundle blocks" which made surgery or relative healing impossible. After this first heart attack I was left with extremely high blood pressure. I lived in fear and was hospitalized constantly. My readings are now normal.

I have on occasions reached the "Tunnel of Death," but somehow survived. I hope you can imagine what this wondrous healing means to me and the magnitude of God's healing power.

I knew immediately that I was the person receiving the healing. I could feel my blood flowing freely through my body. This was previously impossible on account of my circulatory system being "bundle blocked." At the rally I felt warm blood circulating throughout my body. My hands were "on fire" with the warmth of this healing.

I knew I was healed. To verify that I was not being carried away with some fantasy, I decided to request an examination from my doctor. Tests were made: heart, lung x-rays, blood tests.

How my heart was singing, "Alleluia." I knew surprises were in store.

No doubts whatsoever exist. The doctor himself was amazed with my results when he compared it with my previous graphs. There was a remarkable change in the ECG. My "blocked" veins were "opened," allowing the blood to circulate correctly.

The doctor noted my history card with the words, "Remarkable Improvement."

I praise God every minute I can for his Love and Compassion.

A woman's testimony from Louisiana:

On Palm Sunday my husband and I went to the healing service. This particular Sunday my gums were infected. I had throbbing pain and bleeding in my gums. I have had gum infections two or three times before which required oral surgery, cutting away the infected tissues. I prayed for a healing.

When you called out that someone was receiving a healing in the mouth and gums area, I prayed that it would be me. I experienced no heat in the area. The pain was still there.

I continued to pray for healing. You said some were receiving healings and would not be noticed right away. During the celebration of the Eucharist and while receiving the Body of Christ, I kept praying to be healed.

On my way home I noticed the pain was easing and later that night there was even less pain. The next morning the pain was gone completely.

I continue to praise and thank the Lord for this wonderful healing.

Another woman's testimony:

One evening a friend drove me to a neighboring town to attend a healing service. During the service you called out a healing for someone with phlebitis.

I am still thanking and praising the Lord. Up to this day I have not been on any medication.

My doctor's certificate is enclosed.

NOTE: The doctor's certificate states: "No thrombophlebitis since October 1981."

The following is the testimony of a teenager named Karyn Sharkey, age 14. She was healed of an eye condition. This is the letter Karyn wrote to me:

I am writing to you in regard to the healing I received while at your healing service at St. Paul's Church in North Palm Beach, Florida.

Before I went to the service I was praying that my eyes would be healed. My mother told me that tonight is going to be more spiritual healing than physical healing. So I attended just out of curiosity.

I saw miracles being performed in front of everyone's eyes. Doubt was coming into my mind. I then recall, out of the blue, you nonchalantly pointed to the section of the church where I sat. As I looked at you, it seemed as if your finger pointed straight at me. That is when my heart started to pump.

You see, I have had bad vision/astigmatism all my

life. When your hand reached out to the section of the church where I sat, I heard the words come out of your mouth, "A person in this section has distorted vision and is now feeling pressure against your eyes. If this is you, please rise."

As I heard those words come out of your mouth, I felt a tingling sensation in my eyes. I was in my own little world with Jesus. I stood up. You asked me my name, age and how long I had the problem. Tears started to roll down my face as I answered, "I'm Karyn Sharkey. I'm fourteen years old and I have had distorted vision all my life."

I sat down utterly amazed at the experience I'd just been through. Days after I told all my friends and everyone I knew. Some started putting negative feelings in my mind and making me feel unsure. I thank my parents because they kept reassuring me and telling me, "God chose you because of all your faith. He wants you to spread this wonderful happening to everyone."

Mommy told me we had received an appointment card telling me it was time for a checkup the day before the service took place. So the following Tuesday we (my mother and I) went to the eye doctor. He did not know what wonderful thing had occurred in my life. As he looked at my eyes and looked at my file, he said, "Is this the right file? You do have astigmatism, don't you, Karyn?" No reply. Just our laughter. As he kept examining my eyes, he looked puzzled and asked, "Have you had an operation?" I said, "No." Then my mother and I started to laugh and he asked, "What is it?" My mother and I told him what I had experienced. He examined my eyes some more and sat down, while saying, "I'm an atheist, but I believe in what I see. You have 20/20 vision. You can go home and throw away your lens."

After hearing that terrific news we burst out of the office to spread the wonderful blessing and all the blessings of my life.

NOTE: My mother went to the optician's office where my contacts and glasses were made. She asked, "Can Karyn ever have 20/20 vision?" The optician replied, "If she is properly fitted with contacts." My mother said, "I mean without the aid of anything." He said, "It can never be."

My mother proceeded to explain to him what had happened. He said, "She would have to have had two healings — one because of the shape of her eyes and second because of her vision."

I am witnessing this wonderful happening all over the country. May God bless you and all who read this.

Thank you, Karyn, and thanks to all the people who have shared their testimonies of healing with me over the years.

Thank you, Lord, for your signs and wonders among us today.

If we can believe, all things are possible.

EVERYDAY LIFE

To show you that we are moving with the gift of word of knowledge more than we realize, let me address to you a series of questions to see if they ring true for you for some circumstances in your life. Also they will help to illustrate the variety of ways in which word of knowledge is manifested in daily living.

For Music

How many times have you been sitting at a prayer meeting, minding your own business, praising the Lord, when suddenly you get a sense that the song to be sung should be *How Great Thou Art*? The song title, out of nowhere, popped into your thoughts. Someone near you may even say, "I wish we could hear *How Great Thou Art*. Then the song leader immediately begins to sing *How Great Thou Art*. Stunned, you think to yourself, "Gee, isn't that coincidental. That's just the song I was thinking about!" This is a common experience and an example of word of knowledge being manifested through you. It is probably not a coincidence.

It is true that as we are open to the Holy Spirit, the Spirit moves among us. His revelations and manifestations come to the music ministers as well as those in attendance.

Any perceptive music ministry really listening to the Lord will play the songs the Holy Spirit leads them to play. To the music ministers who are reading this, I encourage preparation, but also to be always open to the movement of the Holy Spirit. Listen for his guidance using word of knowledge.

As a music minister opens to using word of knowledge, after a prayer meeting people will sometimes say, "That was just the song I was thinking of when you played it. Thank you. It ministered to me so much." Then, for certain, you will know it was the Lord's guidance because the fruit was good. People were blessed and hearts were touched as they felt the Lord's presence through the music that was played. As this kind of testimony is shared with music ministers, they are affirmed in that they have moved with the Holy Spirit. At gatherings, at prayer meetings, conventions, whatever the function, we come together "as one Body" to move in the Spirit of God.

For Themes or Teachings

How many speakers have had this experience: "I have to teach at a prayer meeting next week. I don't know what to teach," and all of a sudden the word "praise" or some such word comes into your thoughts. In your spirit you know it is right. You think, "I've never taught on that before, but I know it's from the Lord." Then you read up on it, research it, pray about it and deliver your talk. People at the meeting affirm that was what the group needed. You're moving in the Holy Spirit and don't even realize it. We are all moving in the Holy Spirit more than we realize.

At the New York Charismatic Convention in July of 1986, Dick Mishler, a popular speaker in Charismatic Renewal, told this experience to the convention crowd. His experience will support how, through word of knowledge, themes for speaking and teaching are revealed.

This was his experience: He was lying in his bunk asking the Lord what he ought to share at the upcoming conference. Three "words" came to his mind: *weak, worry, weary.* He said to the Lord, "That can't be you, Lord." The Lord revealed this to him, "Dick, that's the way you feel. You feel weak, worried and weary, but when I look into you, that is not what I see." As Dick developed this theme with the people at the convention, he shared that this message was a word from the Lord for everyone, not just for himself.

The Lord further revealed to Dick, "When I look inside you, I do not see that you are weak, worried or weary. Instead I see right to the inside of you. I see that you are *strong, secure* and *steadfast.*" (Praise the Lord! The Lord's vision of us is really different than what we are feeling.)

The words "weak," "worry" and "weary" were words of knowledge given to Dick. As he developed his talk upon those words, it was where the people were at the time. The Lord knew it. Dick had prayerfully sought the Lord's help and the Lord answered his prayer.

Many conference themes have been developed in the same way—through word of knowledge. It comes as an inspiration and revelation from the Holy Spirit. We seek from the Lord his guidance and we should not be surprised when his answers are there!

For Ministries

How many have been talking with a person and the Lord reveals a ministry to you for that person? You hear "ministry with children," or "healing ministry." You sense this with your spirit as a word of knowledge. The Holy Spirit is revealing to you what ministry that person is being called to. This happens frequently in my ministry.

At Prayer Meetings

Have you been at a prayer meeting and repeatedly heard words, such as "backs" in your mind? Then you realize that people's backs are being healed. At that point you can either bring it to the discernment of the core group, or you can pray silently for the completion of that healing.

How many have come into a prayer meeting and the word "depression" comes to mind? You think, "Could there be a lot of depression here? I keep hearing the word depression." At this point it is good to ask the Lord what you could do in the Spirit to help lift the depression.

We should not always speak openly what the Lord is revealing to us. Through the charismatic gift of word of wisdom, we ask the Lord if we are to reveal it. We follow his direction—that's wisdom. Remember word of knowledge and word of wisdom go hand-in-hand.

Perhaps, in the above instance, the Lord revealed to you that you were to pray quietly in the Spirit for the lifting of the heaviness of depression. Your prayer could be that the Lord's light would fill the room dispelling the depression. Silently praying in tongues is another method. Your prayer could also be that the prayer group leader would lead the people into more praise and joyful singing. Anointed praise and worship lift depression. In whichever way the Lord leads you, follow him. The revelation was his — let us also follow his guidance.

With Sacred Scripture

How many have been minding their own business when a chapter and verse of scripture is revealed to you? This is a word of knowledge. The Holy Spirit is giving you a text from scripture that is helpful at that moment.

This also happens frequently during a healing prayer session. A particular scripture passage comes to mind that will be right on target for the other person's needs.

For the Discerning Process

In all the examples I have given thus far I would like to emphasize the need for discernment. We need to ask the Lord, "Lord, is this really your inspiration, your manifestation, your thought in this matter? Is this you, Lord?" We should always seek first that it is indeed the Lord manifesting himself in these situations. The Lord wants us to move in his Holy Spirit even more than we do. If there is any uncertainty, the next proper step would be to check your word of knowledge with your prayer partner or with someone who has a strong gift of discernment. As with most issues in the spiritual realm, we want to move with the balance of the two: with caution that we are not operating out of self; also with confidence that as we have asked the Lord, we shall receive. We move with confidence and caution.

For Work

How many have said, "I really need someone to help me with some work. I don't know who to ask"? You keep hearing a name. It might be the last person you would ask, but you realize it is the person the Lord wants. Then you ask them and they say, "Fine," and all works out well.

Remember the Lord is interested in every facet of our lives — if we but ask him to help, he will.

For Prayer Partners

When prayer partners are praying with each other, ask the Lord what the other needs spiritually. Then pray for that in each other.

Or if there is a block in one's prayer, ask the Lord to reveal what is the root cause of the block and pray through that during your prayer time together.

Members of a prayer meeting core group could also meet to determine if there are any blocks within the prayer meeting. If a member of the core group feels the prayer meeting is not flowing as it should, then meet together to pray. Ask the Lord for the root cause of the block within the prayer meeting. The Lord could reveal that more praise-filled songs are needed. It could be as simple as that. It could be revealed that there is disunity in the core group. Ask the Lord. He will reveal as we ask.

Lost Objects

Have you been in a situation where something has been lost or misplaced? You pray hurriedly, "Lord, where is it? Where did I leave my keys?" Then suddenly you feel you should look in another place where you would not have thought to look before. It is there you find your keys. That's moving in the Holy Spirit with word of knowledge. This makes one realize that the Lord is interested in the smallest details of our lives if we but ask him to help us.

You might ask me, "Okay, Father, that's all well and good. How do we know for certain whether we are moving in the word of knowledge?" My answer to that would be to look for the fruit it bears in one's life or in the prayer group:

1. Does it lead to increased faith in a person's life?

2. Do the songs that the music ministers play really bless the people and lead them into praise?

3. Do we joyfully praise the Lord more when we realize that he has revealed to us the place of a lost object? Does the awareness of the Lord working so intimately in our lives bring us to a greater appreciation of his love?

4. Were the people blessed by the theme of the talk you gave, which was revealed through word of knowledge?

5. Is the person a blessing in the ministry that was revealed for him or her?

6. Were backs really healed when you called out "healing of backs is taking place"?

7. Did the depression at the prayer meeting lift? Did the praise level of the prayer meeting increase after your prayer?

8. Was the person blessed by the position that needed to be filled?

9. Was the shared scripture reading what you needed to sense the Lord's presence and guidance?

10. Do prayer partners grow spiritually as they pray through spiritual blocks?

11. Has the new level of praise in the prayer meeting removed the blocks that were there? Does the meeting flow more in the Spirit?

We look for the *fruit* in the testimony of the people. Word of knowledge will be a blessing both for those through whom it flows and to those receiving it.

When I start to call out the healings that I sense are taking place at a healing service and people's hands go up in response to the word of knowledge, it also increases my faith. To see the Holy Spirit move leads me to more praise in my heart. Word of knowledge bears good fruit in my own life as I see the Lord's blessings upon his people.

In the early days of the Renewal, when I first started to manifest word of knowledge, no one was familiar with this charismatic gift. There were very few who had experienced it.

Now, I would say that 60% of the people in a prayer group have had the experience of word of knowledge. In recent years, openness to charismatic gifts has increased. People are yielding more and more as they sense the movement of the Spirit through them. What I'm saying is, "Go with the Holy Spirit. Move with the Holy Spirit. Go with the flow." The Lord wants to meet the spiritual, physical and emotional needs of his people today.

When the Counsellor comes, whom I shall send
to you from the Father, even the Spirit of truth who
issues from the Father, he will be my witness.
And you too will be witnesses, because you have
been with me from the beginning. (Jn 15:26-27)

Chapter Three

ASPECTS OF INNER HEALING

Inner Healing and Word of Knowledge

In the medical profession healing is basically divided into two parts: diagnosis and therapy. Initially, when a doctor treats a patient's illness, he spends a lot of time listening carefully to the symptoms his patient describes. Then he examines him thoroughly. If he would start treating or prescribing before his diagnosis is complete, there could be serious harm to the patient. So in the medical field the doctor listens and examines, which is part of diagnosis, and then he prescribes the therapy needed.

The charismatic gifts of the Holy Spirit, word of knowledge and word of wisdom, are commonly referred to as the "spiritual diagnosis" and "spiritual prescription" of the inner healing ministry.

The inner healing ministry is that which encompasses the healing of the inner man: emotional, relational, the will and the spiritual. It seems to me we cannot do deep inner healing prayer, or the healing of memories' prayer, without pinpointing the root causes with the charismatic gift of word of knowledge.

The first part of inner healing prayer is diagnosis. This is word of knowledge. We ask the Lord, "Lord, where is the problem? What area in this person's life needs healing? Jesus, I ask you to reveal to me the source of his problem. In what area of this person's life are we to focus our prayer? She wants me to pray for her relationship with her husband," or "He wants me to pray for his problem on the job. Where do his problems really lie? I hear what he is saying, but what are you saying, Lord? Use me as an instrument of your healing for this person."

We begin our prayer with a seeking heart. We move in the Holy Spirit and ask for revelation of root causes. We go right for the root cause of the problem.

When praying with others we have to assume that most people are caught up in the whirlwind of their everyday activities. They frequently cannot perceive that the source of their present-day problems might be rooted in past negative hurts and traumas. Through word of knowledge, the Spirit of God will reveal these root causes to us.

I tell you most solemnly, whoever believes in
me will perform the same works as I do myself,
he will perform even greater works,
because I am going to the Father.
Whatever you ask for in my name I will do,
so that the Father may be glorified in the Son.
(Jn 14:12-13)

So with one ear you are listening to the person and with the other "inner" ear you are listening to what the Lord is revealing.

A woman might want to talk about her mean husband, but the Lord may take you back to a time when she was seven years old. Perhaps there was a divorce in the family, or the father deserted the family. The root cause of her present anger might be that she still has unresolved bitterness and resentment toward her father which carries itself forward to the most significant male in her life now, her husband.

For each person coming for inner healing prayer, we need to ask the Lord specifically for the root cause. Root causes vary from individual to individual. In my ministry I have found that present day problems in relationships are invariably rooted in the past hurts and pains of "primary relationships," often father or mother.

In the situation mentioned above as she is led in a prayer of forgiveness and healing with her father, the present problem with her husband often begins to lessen.

He heals the brokenhearted
and binds up their wounds. (Ps 147:3)

Take the example of the man having difficulty at work. His conflicts could stem from a time in his past when he experienced difficulty with school authorities or teachers. He might have completely forgotten about the past unresolved tension and resentments, but the Holy Spirit may reveal it through word of knowledge.

Then they cried to the Lord in their trouble,
and he delivered them from their distress;
he sent forth his word, and healed them.
(Ps 107:19).

Forgiveness

One of the methods I find helpful and healing after praying with people, is to suggest to them a daily forgiveness program. I ask them to say the Forgiveness Prayer for thirty days. (The Forgiveness Prayer is included as an addendum in the back of the book.) This simple prayer has led many to experience the Lord's love and healing.

The following is a testimony of a woman who committed herself to saying the prayer.

I had a lump on my neck which you prayed over. You had a word of knowledge that I needed to forgive myself. After saying the Forgiveness Prayer daily and having members of my family pray with me — it disappeared.

I went back to the doctor and gave witness to Jesus and to the importance of forgiveness. He was totally amazed. He said he had heard of these healings, but had never really seen one. He realized that maybe he, too, needed to do more forgiving.

Forgiveness, along with inner healing prayer can bring tremendous freedom and healing to us in body, mind and spirit. Frequently we can let go of the events of the past that have remained bottled up and which have "fizzed" inside of us for years. In one sense we can say word of knowledge "pops the top off" and, through forgiveness, all the years of "fizzing resentments" ooze out. As resentment goes out, the light of Jesus can enter in peacefully.

This type of inner healing prayer, focusing on forgiveness, restores joy and lightness to a person's spirit. The light of Jesus Christ is now where resentment once was.

You were darkness once, but now you are
light in the Lord; be like children of light,
for the effects of the light are seen in complete
goodness and right living and truth. (Eph 5:8)

It is wonderful to see this kind of spiritual freedom happening in a person. It is equally wonderful that the Spirit of God is leading us in this day and time to such a fullness of his love.

Indeed, from his fullness we have,
all of us, received . . . (Jn 1:16)

To simplify and clarify the examples I have given under this heading, we might say that word of knowledge is received in answer to the question, "Where is the problem, Lord?" Word of wisdom is received in answer to a follow-up question, "What do we do about it?" or "Where do we go from here?" The Holy Spirit generally reveals the answer to both, if we ask.

The following testimony on forgiveness and inner healing is from the experience of Betty Tapscott, well known international writer and speaker on inner healing:

> Then I started praying for the healing of her painful memories. I asked the Lord to fill the void and give her a mother's and father's love.
>
> We spent several minutes asking the Lord to help her forgive all those who had wounded her. She had been wounded and betrayed by so many people and had to forgive each one.
>
> When we got to age six and the first grade of school, there was such a spirit of darkness, oppression, and loneliness, that I asked, "Jody, what in the world happened then?"
>
> Bless her heart, she started crying as if her heart would break — or more exactly as if a dam had burst and a backlog of filthy, stymied water was finally being released.
>
> When she stopped crying, I asked again, "What happened?"

This was her story.

"Oh, Betty," she said, "we were so poor. We lived on the wrong side of the tracks. We didn't have bathroom facilities or running water. So I went to school dirty, without proper clothes. I never had the right school supplies. None of the kids wanted to play with me — because I was so dirty. Then — to make matters worse — I came down with ringworm, and the doctor and school nurse had to shave my head, and I had to wear a white stocking on my head."

The little girl within her cried and cried as she remembered the teases and taunts of the other kids:

"Get away from us! You're dirty!"

"You've got ringworm! You've got ringworm!"

"We don't want to sit by you. Teacher, make her go away."

On and on and on.

Finally, as her tears subsided, I said, "Jody, Jesus loves you so much. His Word says, 'Lo, I am with you always.' He was there during those awful days. Can you let him love you, take your hand and hold you? He wants to take away the hurt of that horrible memory and give you the love that you so desperately need."

Suddenly she said, "Betty, I see Jesus. He's holding my hand. He wants to be with me. He loves me. I'm not ugly to him. I'm not dirty to him. Oh, I'm beautiful to him."

We hugged each other and rejoiced in the revelation that the Lord had given her.

Then we finished praying the prayer for inner healing. I also made sure that she had been filled with the Holy Spirit.

Then —

For a few moments I just sat back in the chair and looked at the beautiful young woman that God had just transformed who sat before me. Glory!

When she walked back out into the office, everyone was amazed, overjoyed — what a glorious miracle! Hair behind her ears, shoulders erect, a glow on her face, chin held high. Oh, thank you, Lord — what a beautiful self-image!

To finish the story, Jody went back to the university and became a drug counselor. Isn't this story absolutely heavenly? A perfect picture of God's grace, forgiveness, healing and transforming power.[13]

To review briefly the high points of this section:
• The first part of inner healing prayer is word of knowledge. We ask, "Lord, what is the root cause of this person's problem?"
• Word of knowledge is spiritual diagnosis from the Lord.
• The second part of inner healing prayer is word of wisdom. We ask, "Lord, what are we to do?"

[13] Betty Tapscott and Rev. Robert DeGrandis, *Healing of Self-Image* (Tapscott Ministries, P.O. Box 19827, Houston, TX 77224, 1986), pp. 20-4.

- Word of wisdom is spiritual prescription/treatment from the Lord.
- As we are working for the Lord, he is working with us.

- If we ask, we shall receive.
- Jesus desires that we do even greater works than he did (John 14:12).
- Ask the Lord for areas of unresolved conflict in a person's life.
- Look for areas of bitterness, resentment and unforgiveness, especially in primary relationships.
- Present-day problems are invariably rooted in past hurts/traumas.
- Use prayer for forgiveness freely, focusing upon self, others, and the Lord.
- Inner healing brings healing to us on many levels: physically, emotionally, spiritually and relationally.
- As resentments of the past are dealt with, Jesus' light enters and transformation occurs.
- Jesus heals today!

More on Forgiveness

When we pray using word of knowledge, it is very important that the person be open to inner healing. Sometimes a person will become closed to healing prayer on an unconscious level.

This is really possible because the hurt or trauma from the past was so great. What they are really saying is, "I don't want anybody seeing inside my unconscious," and they block you. When a person blocks, it is impossible to get through.

So, occasionally, when you are praying with people you do not receive a word of knowledge. Many times it will be a person's own block which causes this. Focusing on forgiveness is helpful and advised as inner healing frequently begins with for-giveness. My word of knowledge usually relates to forgiveness. Most of my healing ministry is a ministry of forgiveness.

David Duplessis ("Mr. Pentecost") said in a magazine arti-cle in New Covenant that after fifty-two years in the charismatic movement, he considered charismatic gifts of the Holy Spirit and forgiveness two of its most important teachings. I would totally agree on both points.

Working with charismatic gifts we let the Holy Spirit move through us in power and love. Through forgiveness we cleanse and purify our hearts and souls. It's a package program.

Forgiveness is a spiritual law Jesus has given us. We really do not know our own selves entirely when it comes to forgive-ness. No one does. We push hurts into the unconscious mind. Then we deny their existence so we don't have to contend with them. In varying degrees, we all have pockets of unforgiveness and resentment, but we don't realize it.

Sometimes people tell me, "I don't have anyone to forgive," or "I've forgiven everyone I need to forgive." That is probably true on a conscious level. However, most of the time we are contending with buried material.

Some of the questions we might ask ourselves which sug-gest to us that we harbor unforgiveness are these:

Why do I still think angrily about the mean nun in second grade?

Why does that person still upset me every time I think of them?

Why do I want to get even with that repairman who over-charged me?

Is there a situation in my life that I don't want to think or talk about because it causes me too much embarrassment or pain?

Why do we sometimes not return a person's telephone call or avoid places where we know we will see them?

Could it be unforgiveness towards others? Or to ourselves?

Ask the Lord. He will indicate and reveal because he wants us free.

> *. . . forgive us the wrong we have done as*
> *we forgive those who wrong us.* (Mt 6:12)

As you willingly give Jesus permission, people and events that need forgiveness will be brought to your conscious mind. Forgiveness, in one way, is like education: the more you learn, the more you understand how little you know. With forgiveness: the more you are aware of the need to forgive, the more you realize how many you have to forgive. That has been my experience in the healing ministry.

> *Then Peter came up and said to him,*
> *"Lord, how often shall my brother sin against me,*
> *and I forgive him? As many as seven times?"*
> *Jesus said to him,*
> *"I do not say to you seven times,*
> *but seventy times seven."* (Mt 18:21-22)

Even now I am working through difficult areas of my life. My heavenly Father wants to set me free. My heavenly Father wants to heal me because he is love (1 John 4:16). He wants me to experience his love, his salvation, his freedom in the Holy Spirit and his healing even more than I do.

Hopefully you will have an opportunity with your prayer partner or small group to apply some of the ideas I have on word of knowledge, inner healing and forgiveness.

As we yield to charismatic gifts the Lord has given us a beautiful way to minister supernaturally. It is his Way and his Plan. It is exciting to see the Lord moving in such a powerful manner to bring freedom and healing to his people.

As Jesus said at the onset of his active ministry:

The spirit of the Lord has been given to me for he has anointed me. He has sent me to bring good news to the poor, to proclaim liberty to captives and to the blind new sight, to set the downtrodden free, to proclaim the Lord's year of favor. (Lk 4:18-19)

Areas of forgiveness to be aware of:

• Sometimes people are closed on an unconscious level because of deep hurts.

• When this happens, openness is difficult.

• Suggest a daily forgiveness program.

• Time spent focusing on forgiveness will open a person to consciously reveal or talk about deep areas of repressed hurt.

• Through forgiveness we cleanse and purify our hearts.

• Using charismatic gifts we are yielding to the power of the Holy Spirit.

• As ministers of healing we need to put ourselves on a daily program of forgiveness.

• Forgiveness is a spiritual law.

• We all have "pockets" of unforgiveness.

• Jesus wants us free.

• With forgiveness, the more we are aware of the need to forgive, the more we realize how many we have to forgive.

• Jesus calls us to forgive seventy times seven.

The same Spirit of the Lord that was given to Jesus is given to us today, working with us to bring good news to the poor and to set the captives free! It is Jesus channeling his healing love through us.

Jesus also left us with this reminder:

You did not choose me, no, I chose you;
and I commissioned you to go out and bear fruit,
fruit that will last;

and then the Father will give you
anything you ask him in my name.
What I command you is to love one another.
(Jn 15:16-17)

Counseling

In one-on-one counseling much of our time is taken up with listening to the present circumstances or situations of the person. Additionally, we need to pray about any past negative experiences which could be affecting these present situations. I do not mean we should minimize listening to troublesome events in a person's life. Real listening is a gift from the Lord and important to a person's healing. To be open to what the Holy Spirit reveals is also a gift. We need to pray for this balance — with one ear listening to the person and with the other "inner ear" listening to what the Spirit reveals.

One of the most frustrating experiences in my priesthood has been an hour and a half session listening to people's problems without making any headway. Since I have been in the Charismatic Renewal I find that the Holy Spirit, through word of knowledge, can reveal to me the root cause of a person's problem. Then we can begin to pray immediately according to that revelation.

A lot of time and energy can be saved by listening to the Holy Spirit. For effective counseling the Lord will often take you back to childhood because it is there that root causes are most often found.

With this type of "inner" listening and follow-up prayer, I have seen the lasting results of changed lives. In my ministry the fruit has been very good.

Points for counseling:
• Real listening is a gift.
• Listening to what the Lord is revealing is also a gift.
• Pray for this balance in listening: with one ear listening

to the person — with an "inner" ear listening to the Lord.

Spiritual X-Ray

Word of knowledge x-rays the unconscious mind. I have friends that tell me I should not be doing this. They say, "You're taking too much into your own hands. What you're teaching and giving people is spiritual x-ray. Sooner or later, someone is going to abuse it." I admit that sometimes this does happen.

I have trained people in many parts of the country to use word of knowledge. Occasionally, reports come back to me that they have been praying with people like this: "Jesus, bless this person. Help him to stop drinking." As these people are praying, the Holy Spirit has revealed, through word of knowledge, that the person being prayed for has a drinking problem. Remember what I mentioned earlier about asking the Lord what we are to do once we receive a word of knowledge. We should not always state openly what we have received through word of knowledge. Sometimes we should say a prayer of blessing, such as, "Lord, bless this person in mind, body and spirit. We thank you for his life. Lord Jesus, let your healing love flow through him in a mighty way. Touch and cleanse all the deep areas in his life that need to be filled with your healing love. Thank you, Lord Jesus, for what you are doing within him right at this moment."

This way we are not invading the person's privacy. We need to move carefully in the delicate areas of a person's life. Of course, if they want to pray about the root causes of their drinking, then that is different.

We wouldn't start praying in tongues out loud during a parish Mass, which is non-charismatic, would we? Of course not. Prudence also needs to be exercised, even more particularly with word of knowledge, because we're dealing with such deep levels of a person's being. Mistakes will happen and abuses will occur. We should strive to minimize them as much as we can.

Once I was praying with a woman and I received the words "unforgiveness" and "husband."

I asked her, "Is there any possibility of unforgiveness in your family?"

"Oh, no, Father. I love all my family," she replied.

"Any resentment toward your husband perhaps?" I asked her.

"Oh, no. No, he's a loving man," she replied back.

I knew in my spirit what the Lord had revealed. So I prayed instead of confronting her. I lifted up to the Lord the whole situation. I knew she was not ready to admit any act of unforgiveness toward her husband. Many times this occurs as people are unwilling to confess unforgiveness toward their spouse or loved ones. They consider this an admission of disloyalty or unlove.

It is often difficult to admit that one's parents or spouse has inflicted hurt or pain on us. We have all been hurt by loved ones. We've got to face the truth of this. Most of the time it will be the people who are closest to us who will inflict the most pain. It is precisely because we are in close contact with them that this happens.

Husbands need to forgive their wives; wives need to forgive husbands; parents need to forgive their children; children need to forgive their parents; brothers need to forgive their sisters; sisters need to forgive their brothers; friends need to forgive friends; employees need to forgive their employers; people need to forgive the Church; students need to forgive their teachers; teachers need to forgive their students. The list is limitless. To extend forgiveness to loved ones or associates is not a disloyal act — forgiveness is a loving act! For more testimonies on how forgiveness is loving I refer you to my book, *Healing the Broken Heart.*[14]

---

[14] Robert DeGrandis, S.S.J., *Healing the Broken Heart* (HOM Books, 108 Aberdeen Street, Lowell, MA 01850), 1989.

To condense:

- Word of knowledge x-rays the unconscious mind.
- It is a spiritual x-ray.
- Ask the Lord if you are to reveal openly what he has revealed to you through word of knowledge.
- Respect a person's privacy. Use prudence and wisdom.
- Sometimes only a prayer of blessing is desirable.
- People find it difficult to admit to family unforgiveness.

Chapter Four

GENERAL PRINCIPLES
A SUMMARY OF THE WORD
OF KNOWLEDGE

1. Charismatic gifts are for everyone as a result of being baptized in the Holy Spirit.

> *. . . unless a man is born through water and*
> *the Spirit, he cannot enter the kingdom of God:*
> *what is born of the flesh is flesh;*
> *what is born of the Spirit is spirit.*
> (Jn 3:5-6)

The Lord supplies us, through charismatic gifts with the means and power to do his work because, as you recall, it is the ministry of Jesus through us. If we are to follow the injunction of Mk 16:17 in which we are called to "lay hands on the sick, speak in other tongues and cast out spirits," then working with charismatic gifts is imperative.

If we specifically address the deliverance ministry, which is the casting out of evil spirits and infilling with the Holy Spirit, the revelational gifts are especially imperative. To know there is the presence of an evil spirit, we rely on the charismatic gift of discernment. To know its name, we rely on word of knowledge and following the directions given by the Lord through word of wisdom, we bind and cast it out.

An example: First we discern (gift of discernment) the presence of an evil spirit. Then we ask and seek from the Lord the type of evil spirit, its specific name (gift of word of knowledge). Specific identification of the spirit will give us more power over it precisely because we are not dealing in generalities. The Lord might reveal to you through word of knowledge "spirit of fear." Then you can bind and cast the spirit out as the Lord leads (word of wisdom). All these works are the manifestation of the Holy Spirit through us.

Before we proceed in anything as serious as deliverance, we should be familiar with healing prayer and have the guidance of someone experienced in this ministry. Especially in deliverance we rely on the Holy Spirit's guidance, not our own. We ask the Lord, "How do I handle this? Do I tell the person what I am sensing? Do I not tell the person? Do I pray quietly? Do I suggest that they go to the sacrament of Reconciliation? Do I do the deliverance now?" So we need the charismatic revelational gifts particularly for the very injunction of Mark 16:17 to cast out demons.

2. The charismatic gift of word of knowledge helps to build the Body of Christ.

Now to each one the manifestation of the Spirit
is given for the common good.
(1 Cor 12:7)

Word of knowledge works in many ways for the common good. One of the most practical, loving ways is when we are praying with people. People generally do not know the root causes of their own problems, so we ask the Lord.

Recently I had a case where a girl said she had temptations

to suicide. From the very onset of our conversation while she was telling me of her suicidal temptations, I was asking the Lord silently for the root cause and the "word" I received from the Lord was "ancestral." I then asked her if suicidal tendencies ran in her family. She said, "Yes." So I prayed with her asking the Lord to cut off any genetic ties with her past generations. The knowledge of this family tendency to suicide came from the revelation of the Lord. I did not know this of myself.

Word of knowledge is the best way to get to root problems. We are really ministering more effectively. It is not a superficial judgment that we are making about a person; it is revelation from the Holy Spirit.

Word of knowledge does help to build the Body of Christ because the Lord is using you, manifesting himself through you to set his people free. He is using you to do something for people they probably never would have been able to do for themselves.

Let us move with the assurance that word of knowledge is divinely ordained by the Lord to build his Body as he continues his ministry through us.

> *I tell you most solemnly, whoever believes in me*
> *will perform the same works as I do myself,*
> *he will perform even greater works,*
> *because I am going to the Father.*
> (John 14:12)

3. Word of knowledge reveals facts that are unknown.

> *. . . when he, the Spirit of truth, comes,*
> *he will guide you into all truth.*
> *He will not speak on his own;*
> *he will speak only what he hears,*
> *and he will tell you what is yet to come.*
> (Jn 16:13)

For example, sometimes I may be praying with a person pertaining to ministry and the Lord will give me a "word" about that person. The word "healing" might come to mind. Then I say, "I heard the Lord saying you have a strong gift of healing." Sometimes people are surprised as they answer, "I've been seeing things happening as I pray with people, but I have been doubting this gift." In this case they had the awareness that healings were happening, but they doubted. The word I gave is a confirmation to them.

Word of knowledge reveals facts that are unknown. In earlier chapters I gave many examples:

(1) what songs the music ministers are to play
(2) to reveal topics and themes to speakers and teachers
(3) to reveal ministries or special gifts
(4) to reveal healings taking place during healing services
(5) for selection of leaders
(6) for scripture readings during a healing prayer session
(7) to reveal areas of spiritual blocks for prayer partners
(8) for revealing negative root causes for a person's physical, psychological or spiritual illness — the cause of illness
(9) to reveal facts for everyday living
(10) for inner healing prayer sessions
(11) for leaders to identify difficulties during a prayer meeting
(12) for revealing the person or persons we need to forgive

In all of these examples facts are given by the Holy Spirit which were previously unknown to the one praying for healing.

I might add that the list could be limitless as to the ways in which the Spirit moves. These are the more specific ways in which I have experienced word of knowledge in my ministry and the experiences of ministers/friends. I am sure as time goes on the Lord will reveal more and more ways in which this healing charismatic gift operates. We cannot limit the Lord!

4. Word of knowledge is God's diagnosis.

> *In fact God, who can read everyone's*
> *heart . . .* (Acts 15:8).
> *. . . and God who knows everything in our*
> *hearts. . .* (Rom 8:27).

Man looks at the exterior. God looks at the heart. The Lord sees the inside of us, into our inner being. Because he can see to the core of us, he can reveal areas that we would never have come to the knowledge of ourselves. The Lord knows us more than we know ourselves.

For example, recently there was a man having a terrible trauma because of fear of a nervous breakdown. As I prayed with him, I heard the word "wife." As it came out his wife was pushing him to take a new job. Unconsciously he had a fear of having a nervous breakdown that his father had once had. He could never have put that together. He and his wife had a good marriage. The fact that they had a good marriage just obscured the truth. Unconsciously he was afraid that the added responsibility of a new job would bring him to a nervous breakdown, which is where he experienced fear.

The Lord just zeroed in on the problem. The one he never would expect and the person he loved the most was adding to his own problem of fear of a nervous breakdown.

The principle is that we generally do not know the root cause of our own problems. We are too close.

5. Word of knowledge is part of normal Christianity.

> *. . . while they, going out, preached everywhere,*
> *the Lord working with them and confirming the*
> *word by the signs that accompanied it.*
> (Mk 16:20)

If we believe that we are called to heal the sick daily, then we can believe that word of knowledge is part of normal Christianity.

It is our commission as disciples of Jesus to fulfill the injunction of Mark 16:17 to heal the sick. Usually 80% of the people coming for healing prayer for physical ailments are suffering from illnesses caused by tension and stress; therefore we should get to the emotional root.

6. Word of knowledge enables the ministry of Jesus to flow through us.

> *I tell you most solemnly, whoever believes in me*
> *will perform the same works as I do myself,*
> *he will perform even greater works,*
> *because I am going to the Father.*
> *Whatever you ask for in my name I will do,*
> *so that the Father may be glorified in the Son.*
> (Jn 14:12-13)

The sacrament of Confirmation is a continuation of Jesus' ministry through us. Scripture reveals that Jesus sent the twelve. That was not enough, so he sent seventy-two. That was not enough, so he sent 120 at Pentecost. That was not enough, so he poured out his Spirit on all flesh. The same Holy Spirit that was in Jesus is in us. The same Holy Spirit continues the ministry of Jesus through us.

Fr. James McManus, C.SS.R., in his book *The Healing Power of the Sacraments,* states this:

> For a long time I could not really accept these words
> of Christ. I would say to myself, "How can anyone do
> a greater work than Jesus, the Son of God?" I was
> attributing all the works of Jesus to his divinity. He
> was divine, and therefore he worked all those mira-
> cles; we are only human, so how can we do the same

works that he did? All the time I was missing the central truth revealed in the ministry of Jesus. What he did, he did through the power of the Holy Spirit. And he has given that same Holy Spirit to us.[15]

7. Word of knowledge is necessary for inner healing.

Peace I bequeath to you, my own peace I give you,
a peace the world cannot give, this is my gift to you.
(Jn 14:27)

Because 90% of the human mind is unconscious, we do not know all that is within us and sometimes we do not even suspect what is there. For example, Ruth Carter Stapleton stated in her book, *The Experience of Inner Healing,* that the parent that you think you need to forgive is generally the wrong one. It was her experience that the opposite is true. You can see how confused we can be.

We need the Lord to guide us like a plane landing on a runway during foggy weather. A pilot would find it difficult to find it unless he listened to the directions from tower control. With the assistance of the controllers, the difficulty is lessened. The controllers can see the plane on the radar screen, and bring the pilot right to the end of the runway no matter how thick the fog is. It is the same with the Spirit of God. When we listen, he will bring us and direct us to root causes of illness. We cannot "see," but he does. We just listen.

8. Everyone has a healing gift by virtue of the baptism in the Spirit, but some have a ministry of healing and therefore especially need word of knowledge.

And as you go, proclaim that the kingdom
of heaven is close at hand.
Cure the sick, raise the dead,

[15] Jim McManus, C.SS.R., *The Healing Power of the Sacraments* (Notre Dame, Indiana 46556: Ave Maria Press, 1984), p. 21.

cleanse the lepers, cast out devils.
(Mt 10:7-8)

Many ministers have healing services, using the gift of word of knowledge as part of their ministry, as I myself have. We give words of knowledge as we believe we hear or see them from the Lord. Many, many people have that gift. They have a ministry of healing and the Lord gives them, during a special anointed time, word of knowledge so they can sense the healings that are occurring during the healing service.

In Fr. Ralph DiOrio's book, *A Miracle to Proclaim,* there are many examples that attest to such healings during his services. I quote one of them that directly pertains to the manifestation of the gift of word of knowledge:

I sent for thirty tickets for the November 28, 1981, healing service, as our family and friends wanted to go. We felt excited to share the service with all of the people whom we love. About two hours after the service began, I experienced pins and needles in my lower abdomen. I also felt very warm. Then Father DiOrio received 'word of knowledge' that a woman dressed in orchid clothing was being healed of a problem in her Fallopian tubes. I looked around to see the person stand up and then realized that it was myself. I was wearing an orchid sweater and was so hot! The girl next to me said that I was radiating heat to her. At that moment my mother looked at me and said, "Chris, it's you." An usher walked to me and I stood up. Then Father DiOrio looked right at me and said, "That's the young lady. Come up here." I walked up to the stand and Father told me that I was being completely healed. He prayed with me and I was slain in the Spirit. When I woke up, I knew that Jesus had healed me, but I never dreamed that, one month later to the day, I would find out that I was pregnant.

My husband and I jumped for joy when the nurse said, "It's positive!" Then we cried. We were so happy! We called everyone that we knew to tell them the good news. Many of my friends had been doubters because my healing could not be seen. They had said, "When you get pregnant, then we'll believe." Well, now I was calling to tell them of my miracle.[16]

Fr. DiOrio has a recognized ministry of healing using the charismatic gift of word of knowledge. However, we are all called to move daily in the power of the Holy Spirit.

9. Word of knowledge comes in many ways: vision, words, feelings, sacred scripture readings.

> *There is a variety of gifts but always the same Spirit;*
> *there are all sorts of service to be done,*
> *but always to the same Lord; working*
> *in all sorts of different ways in different people,*
> *it is the same God who is working in all of them.*
> (1 Cor 12:4-6)

Vision: as cited before, Father DiOrio has the picture of the person being healed and he can describe them, even to the clothing they are wearing. Sometimes he can name them.

Words: I hear "words" in my mind during healing services and I know it is the Lord revealing the healings that are taking place, such as, *hearts, backs, cancer* or *eyes.*

Feelings: some people get a feeling of pain in a particular

---

[16] Fr. Ralph A. DiOrio, *A Miracle to Proclaim* (Garden City, New York: Image Books, a division of Doubleday & Company, Inc., 1984), pp.86-7.

area and they know someone there has an ailment in that same area that is being touched and healed by the Lord.

Sacred scripture: some just open scripture and the Lord will give them a word in scripture relevant to the healing that needs to take place in the community.

10. There is continued growth in all the gifts, especially word of knowledge.

a. Pray and ask the Lord for the gift. Desire the gift.

b. Read about it and learn as much as we can from other people. Word of knowledge can be experienced in many ways with different people.

c. If you meet someone who has a strong gift of word of knowledge, ask them to pray over you for a greater release of the gift.

In 1971, I met a minister who saw colors and could tell what was going on in a person by the color he saw around them. I asked him to pray over me and he did. He laughed when I asked him to do this. I never could figure out why he laughed except that he was thinking that I was going to get what I asked for. My word of knowledge did not develop that way. It did come through "words." Constantly I am open to the way in which the Lord wishes to move and if the Lord wants to reveal colors to me, he will and I will be grateful.

11. Word of knowledge has an evangelical effect.

Come and see someone who told
me everything I ever did!
(Jn 4:29)

Giving a word of knowledge to someone often makes them a believer and also those who witness it. In instances when I have prayed with a person individually and I have given them a "word" they were really shocked that another person would have insight into their inner workings. They know right away that what has been revealed has to be from the Lord. Many times a word of knowledge which I have given to a person is just what they needed to enable them to discuss past situations or traumas which, perhaps, they have never been able to discuss freely with anyone before. Many, many people open up to past hurts and traumas in this way. It really helps them to believe in the power of the Lord working through people. One time I heard the word "rage". The woman was shocked because she had never told anyone of this experience.

John Wimber of Vineyard Ministries uses the example of a woman who denied she needed to forgive anyone. He said, "Do you need to forgive your sister?" and she said, "How do you know that?" So she knew God was working through him revealing this area of unforgiveness in her life.

The example of the scripture story of the Samaritan woman at the well as we explained in an earlier chapter is a shining example of the evangelical effect that word of knowledge has upon people. We called it the "ripple effect."

> Many Samaritans of that town had believed in him on the strength of the woman's testimony when she said, "He told me all I have ever done," so when the Samaritans came up to him, they begged him to stay with them. He stayed for two days, and when he spoke to them many more came to believe; and they said to the woman, "Now we no longer believe because of what you told us; we have heard him ourselves and we know that he really is the savior of the world". (Jn 4:39-42)

12. Priests can often use this gift in confession and counseling.

> *For those whose sins you forgive, they are forgiven;*
> *for those whose sins you retain, they are retained.*
> (Jn 20:23)

Generally when you are in close contact with people, one-on-one, and they are open to you and you are open to them, word of knowledge will occur. This happens especially in the sacrament of Reconciliation. I've heard many, many priests say that they get inspirations and revelations from the Holy Spirit while hearing a person's confession. I suspect they are words of knowledge revealing sins that a person doesn't confess.

I remember once I visited a man dying of cancer and as I was praying with him the Lord revealed to me his past sin of adultery. I asked him tactfully, "Have you ever committed a serious sin that is unconfessed?" He said, "Yes, I have." I then said, "You need to include that in your confession." He died a few days later, but I am sure that was helpful to prepare him.

13. Word of knowledge points out barriers to God's love.

I have come so that they may have life
and have it to the full.
(Jn 10:10)

Inner healing, as a rule, removes some of the barriers to God's love. It also points out areas where people need to repent, areas they were not specifically aware of. For example, if someone has an envious spirit, you can pick that up through word of knowledge. They may know themselves to be envious, but they don't realize how serious it is. What the Lord is saying as he reveals this to you is that it is more serious than even they realize. They really need to work on it and receive more inner healing in this area, by working on the root causes.

Unforgiveness and resentment are perhaps the clearest examples of a negativity which blocks us and is a barrier to God's love. Again the very fact that the Lord reveals this repeatedly shows us the importance of forgiveness in our lives.

14. Word of knowledge is helpful to find who we need to forgive.

. . . unless you each forgive
your brother from your heart
(Mt 18:35)

The Lord has forgiven you;
now you must do the same.
(Col 3:13).

I tell you therefore: everything you ask and pray for,
believe that you have it already, and it will be yours.
And when you stand in prayer,
forgive whatever you have against anybody,
so that your Father may forgive your failings too.
(Mk 11:25)

On a final note we really need to ask the Lord who we need to forgive because most people cannot remember who hurt them in their younger years. The little child that we were still lives within us and must be dealt with.

Chapter Five

WORD OF KNOWLEDGE WORKSHOP AND PRAYERS

Once I facilitated a workshop on the charismatic gift of word of knowledge for members of the Association of Christian Therapists. In this group there was a psychologist who was a department head of a state hospital. That workshop, he later told me, revolutionized his whole practice of psychology. It encouraged him to see that balance that I spoke of earlier: listening to the person, but also listening to the Holy Spirit through the use of the charismatic gifts he has given us.

In a word of knowledge workshop I encourage people to yield to and move in this important healing gift. When I conduct a workshop, I tell them about my experience with it and then get them actively involved using the following format:

1. To begin I have the people form a circle.

2. They place their hands on the person's shoulder to their right.

3. Then we pray softly in tongues to keep our minds clear and focused on Jesus.

4. Then we listen in silence.

5. We ask the Lord to reveal a "word of knowledge" to us for the person we are praying for.

6. The Lord will often give a word, a picture, a sense, an image or an emotion. Remember this will be a symbol of a negative trauma that needs to be healed.

7. We first share with the person to our right the word we have received for them. We wait for their response.

8. We pray with each other for whatever healing is needed.

Once in a workshop a woman received a word of "unloving" for the person to her right. The other woman immediately responded and said she knew what that meant. She said she had always felt that her mother did not love her. She had no problem relating to that word right away. The word "unloving" was a symbol of a lack of love, indicating a relationship that needed healing. We were then led to pray for healing of her relationship with her mother using forgiveness. She felt much better after that.

The following are examples of a word of knowledge workshop and testimonies as given by my sister, Dorothea DeGrandis Sudol:

Once I was giving a word of knowledge workshop to a group of leaders. Again I stressed the fact it was not a toy. We were to use this gift with sensitivity, wisdom and prudence.

The following week I was absent. They were praying with a priest who had not been present at our word of knowledge workshop. Well, they had some words of knowledge over him. They spoke them right out to him. He became very irritated. In fact, he was angry. You see, he didn't know what it was all about. That's why I caution people to be very, very careful.

I usually ask people's permission, "May I use the word of knowledge as I pray?" Then if they don't know what I am talking about I explain it to them.

An example of word of knowledge: it could be that you get the word "window." You ask the person you are praying with, "What does window mean to you?" They might say, "I don't know. That doesn't mean anything to me." They can't relate to it then. Still trust your word of knowledge. You've asked the Lord and he is going to give it to you. Even if they can't relate to the word, I still always pray for the healing. I say, "Thank you, Jesus, for your word of knowledge. Lord, we ask you to heal that area in which this word is symbolic. You know what it means. I ask you to go back into that memory and heal, touch and make whole. Amen."

Someone shared with me recently her experience with word of knowledge. Someone, during a workshop, had gotten the word "bridge" over her. They asked her what it meant. They even had a vision with this. They saw lightning, heard the thunder and could see two children walking over a broken bridge.

They prayed about the word and nothing seemed to come. The next month I was back in the same area again. This woman said, "I went home and asked my mother about this vision. I was telling her about the word of knowledge workshop. My mother related to the word right away." It appears this young woman and her little boy cousin when they were children had wandered away from a family picnic. They were at a park. A sudden thunderstorm came up and the two children did lose their way and the grownups had to go find them over the bridge. This word was a symbol of a trauma that needed healing.

I remember a word I once got over my own brother.

The word was "paper." The Lord even went further and revealed "parchment paper." I visualized it as old and sort of yellowish. He identified right away with it. He said, "Oh, I know what that is. In grandmother's house, in her living room, was a picture of this man with a scowl on his face. He had a black handlebar mustache and a black derby on." My brother said every time he went into my grandmother's living room that picture frightened him. I told him that it never bothered me. In fact, every time I went through the living room I stuck my tongue out at him.

See how different people react to different situations. It scared him, but it didn't scare me.

One time I got the words "boiling water" over someone. The woman I was praying for identified with it. Boiling water had once tipped over on the stove and scalded her. She had to be isolated in one of the back rooms of the house as her burns were healing. She felt alone and rejected in the back of the house. We prayed through this time in her life and she felt better.

When we speak the word of knowledge it is the power of the Lord in operation. When we are praying with people we ask the Lord for root causes. This is when word of knowledge is very beneficial.

The more we experience God's love in inner healing, the more we love ourselves. The more we love ourselves, the more we can love others. We cannot give away what we do not have inside ourselves.

You will not truly understand inner healing until you experience it for yourself. We have tools when we are ministering with others—the tools are the gifts of the Holy Spirit. We need them because we are in spiritual warfare and we need all the help we can get. We are all broken people, wounded healers. If you are a member of the human race, you need inner healing.

This gift is not a toy. It must be used with love, sensitivity, wisdom and prudence.[17]

When people begin to yield to word of knowledge, for example, in a workshop setting, the person receiving the word might say, "Hey, that doesn't mean anything to me." You might, at this point, begin to doubt what the Lord has revealed. Don't doubt. Be patient, pray and wait. Trust the "word" you believe the Lord has given you for that person. Usually within a short period of time they will come back and say, "Oh, now I know what that word meant. It just dawned on me."

What happens is that the memory comes from the unconscious to the conscious level. The person is then able to relate to it. Sometimes there are layers of memories that are painful. People keep them repressed. They are not ready to look at the negative event or are unable to handle the pain associated with it.

There's a natural tendency to doubt your gifts. Resist that. Through the years I've learned to trust the gifts the Lord has given me. If in doubt, ask your prayer partner to confirm your gift.

[17] Dorothea DeGrandis Sudol, *Word of Knowledge* cassette (108 Aberdeen Street, Lowell, MA 01850).

An example of this is once while I was working with a counselor and I received the words "burning" and "fire."

He said, "I can't relate to that."

I said, "Okay. Just pray about it and see if something will surface."

I knew it was a word from the Lord because not only did I hear a word, but I received a vision at the same time.

Two weeks later I received a letter from the counselor which stated, "I finally remembered what that was. I was counseling with a woman for four years. She was suicidal and she burned herself to death by pouring fluid over herself and then ignited it."

The painful memory did not surface immediately. It took two weeks. It was too painful for him to remember. In my own ministry I had a similar occurrence with a suicide.

The Lord wants to heal all of our painful memories of negative past events, wanting to set us free from all guilt, fear, resentment and unforgiveness, especially toward ourselves.

When you receive your first word of knowledge or even after that, you will probably say, "Is that really me or is that the Lord?" It is here we have to move in faith to trust that once we have prayed, then we will receive a true word of knowledge.

When we are operating on a faith dimension, it may be difficult for us to step out and say it is the Lord. It all seems too simple. We might say, "It has to be harder than this!" In reply I say, "The things of man tend to be complicated. The things of God tend to be simple. Simple, but not easy!"

Prayers for Release of Word of Knowledge

The following prayers should be an integral part of any Word of Knowledge workshop and can be prayed by those who feel drawn to exercising this gift of the Holy Spirit. Prayer 2 is especially helpful as an ongoing prayer for all those who are using this gift to heal and build the Body.

Prayer 1

Thank you, Jesus, for the gift of life and for the gift of your Holy Spirit who moves through us in so many powerful ways, especially through charismatic gifts.

We ask that, as we surrender ourselves to you, the Holy Spirit give himself to us. Today we particularly pray for the release of the gift of word of knowledge within us. Jesus, we yield ourselves to you. We pray for an outpouring and anointing of your Spirit upon us.

Lord Jesus, we pray —

That as we pray with others, root causes of a person's illness, sickness or bondage be revealed. Set us free, Lord Jesus.

That we also may be open to know the healings that are taking place in a community. We ask for the wisdom and grace to know when and how we are to share this knowledge for the greater good of all. Teach us, Lord.

That in the everyday experiences of our lives we may be open to your guidance through word of knowledge. Lead us in your ways.

Thank you, Jesus, for the many ways, beyond our understanding, in which this gift will be manifested through us. We are grateful that as we ask we receive and are enabled to move in and with the power of your Holy Spirit.

In Jesus' name, we pray.

Prayer 2

Lord Jesus, I know that you have blessed me to be your disciple. You say, "My Father's glory is shown by your bearing much fruit; and in this way you become my disciples" (John 15:8). Lord Jesus, I want to bear fruit for you through the use of the gift of word of knowledge. I want to use this gift to help heal and build up the Body of Christ.

Please remove any obstacles to the release of this gift, Lord. I ask your forgiveness for any time I have not been willing to receive a word through a particular person, because of negative feelings towards that individual. I extend forgiveness to those individuals who have used this gift without wisdom, and caused confusion or harm. I ask your forgiveness for being afraid of using the gift—afraid of being rejected, ridiculed, or simply afraid of being wrong.

For any way that these responses have blocked the flow of this gift in my own ministry, I am truly sorry. I receive your forgiveness, Lord, and I forgive myself.

I ask now to be totally open to the use of this gift. Touch me, Jesus, and release in me the gift of word of knowledge and a gift of your wisdom to know how to act upon the words that you give. Please provide opportunities for me to exercise this gift.

Lord, I believe that your Holy Spirit is working in me more than I realize. Please help me to be more sensitive to what you are already doing. Thank you, Lord Jesus, for the many ways beyond my understanding, in which this gift will be manifested through me. I pray for an outpouring and anointing of your Spirit upon me. AMEN.

Forgiveness Prayer

The following prayer covers most of the significant areas of forgiveness. Often, such a prayer will bring to mind other areas that need forgiveness. Let the Holy Spirit move freely and guide your mind to persons or groups that you need to forgive.

Lord Jesus Christ, I ask today to forgive everyone in my life. I know that you will give me the strength to forgive. I thank you that you love me more than I love myself and want my happiness more than I desire it for myself.

Father, I forgive YOU for the times death has come into the family, hard times, financial difficulties, or what I thought were punishments sent by you. When people said, "It is God's will," I became bitter and resentful toward you. Purify my heart and mind today.

Lord, I forgive MYSELF for my sins, faults and failings; for all that is bad in me or that I think is bad, I forgive myself. For any delvings in superstition, using ouija boards, horoscopes, going to seances, using fortune telling or wearing lucky charms, I reject all that superstition and choose you alone as my Lord and Savior. Fill me with your Holy Spirit.

I further forgive myself for taking your name in vain, using drugs, not worshipping you by attending church, for hurting my parents, getting drunk, for sins against purity, bad books, bad movies, fornication, adultery, homosexuality. Also for abortion, stealing, lying, defrauding, hurting people's reputations. You have forgiven me. Today I forgive myself.

I truly forgive my MOTHER. I forgive her for all the times she hurt me, resented me, was angry with me and for all the times she punished me. I forgive her for the times she preferred my brothers and sisters to me. I forgive her for the times she told me I was dumb, ugly, stupid, the worst of the children or that I cost the family a lot of money. Also for the times she told me I was unwanted, an accident, a mistake or not what she expected, I forgive her.

I forgive my FATHER. I forgive him for any nonsupport, any lack of love, affection or attention. I forgive him for any lack of time, for not giving me his companionship, for his drinking, arguing and fighting with my mother or the other children. For his severe punishments, for desertion, for being away from home, for divorcing my mother or any running around, I do forgive him.

Lord, I extend forgiveness to my SISTERS and BROTHERS. I forgive those who rejected me, lied about me, hated me, resented me, competed for my parents' love, those who hurt me, who physically harmed me. For those who were too severe on me, punished me or made my life unpleasant in any way, I do forgive them.

Lord, I forgive my SPOUSE for lack of love, affection, consideration, support, attention, communication; for faults, failings, weaknesses and those other acts or words that hurt or disturb me.

Jesus, I forgive my CHILDREN for their lack of respect, obedience, love, attention, support, warmth, understanding; for their bad habits, falling away from the church, any bad actions which disturb me.

My God, I forgive my IN-LAWS, my MOTHER-IN-LAW, FATHER-IN-LAW, SON/DAUGHTER-IN-LAW and OTHER RELATIVES by marriage who treat my family with a lack of love. For all their words, thoughts, actions or omissions which injure and cause pain, I forgive them.

Please help me forgive my RELATIVES, my GRANDMOTHER and GRANDFATHER, AUNTS, UNCLES, COUSINS who have interfered in our family, been possessive of my parents, who may have caused confusion or turned one parent against the other.

Jesus, help me to forgive my CO-WORKERS who are disagreeable or make life miserable for me. For those who push their work off on me, gossip about me, won't cooperate with me, try to take my job, I do forgive them.

My NEIGHBORS need to be forgiven, Lord. For all their noise, letting their property run down, not tying up their dogs who run through my yard, not taking in their trash barrels, being prejudiced and running down the neighborhood, I do forgive them.

I now forgive all PRIESTS, NUNS, PARISH MEMBERS, PARISH COUNCIL MEMBERS, PARISH ORGANIZATION HEADS, my PASTOR, the BISHOP, the POPE and the ROMAN CATHOLIC CHURCH for their lack of support, affirmation, leadership, bad sermons, pettiness, lack of friendliness, not providing me or my family with the inspiration we needed, for any hurts they have inflicted upon me or my family—even in the distant past—I forgive them today.

Lord, I forgive all those who are of different PERSUASIONS, those of opposite political views who have attacked me, ridiculed me, discriminated against me, made fun of me, economically hurt me.

I forgive those of different religious DENOMINATIONS who have tried to convert me, harrassed me, attacked me, argued with me, forced their views on me.

Those who have harmed me ETHNICALLY, have discriminated against me, mocked me, made jokes about my race or nationality, hurt my family physically, emotionally or economically, I do forgive them today.

Lord, I forgive all PROFESSIONAL PEOPLE who have hurt me in any way: doctors, nurses, lawyers, judges, politicians and civil servants. I forgive all SERVICE PEOPLE; policemen, firemen, bus drivers, hospital workers and especially repairmen who have taken advantage of me in their work.

Lord, I forgive my EMPLOYER for not paying me enough money, for not appreciating my work, for being unkind and unreasonable with me, for being angry or unfriendly, for not promoting me, and for not complimenting me on my work.

Lord, I forgive my SCHOOL TEACHERS and INSTRUCTORS of the past as well as the present. For those who punished me, humiliated me, insulted me, treated me unjustly, made fun of me, called me dumb or stupid, made me stay after school, I truly forgive them today.

Lord, I forgive my FRIENDS who have let me down, lost contact with me, did not support me, were not available when I needed help, borrowed money and did not return it, gossiped about me.

Lord Jesus, I especially pray for the grace of forgiveness for that ONE PERSON in life who has HURT ME THE MOST. I ask to forgive anyone whom I consider my greatest enemy, the one who is the hardest to forgive or the one I said I would never forgive.

Lord, I beg pardon of all these people for the hurt I have inflicted on them, especially my mother and father, and my marriage partner. I am especially sorry for the three greatest hurts I have inflicted on each.

Thank you, Jesus, that I am being set free of the evil of unforgiveness. Let your Holy Spirit fill me with light and let every dark area of my mind be enlightened. AMEN.

NOTE:

Forgiveness is an act of the will, not a feeling. If we pray for a person, we can be assured that we have forgiven that person.

To help accept an individual and open ourselves to a particular person more, visualize them with the Lord Jesus. Say to the Lord, "I love them because you love them."

Forgiveness is a lifelong obligation.

Daily we need to forgive those who hurt or injure us.

This is my commandment:
love one another as I have loved you.
(Jn 15:12)

Deliverance Prayer

The following prayer can be very effective when prayed by anyone who has been involved with any form of worship or influence that is apart from God and the power of Jesus Christ.

Allow the Holy Spirit to enlighten you as to their danger and protect you from any further involvement.

I place myself in the presence of Jesus Christ and submit to him as Lord and Savior. I put on God's armor to resist the devil's tactics. I stand my ground with truth buckled around my waist, and integrity for a breastplate. I carry the shield of faith to put out the burning arrows of the evil one. I accept salvation from God to be my helmet and receive the word of God from the Spirit to use as a sword (Eph 6:10,11,14,16,17).

In the name of Jesus Christ I reject Satan and all of his works. I reject every power apart from God and every form of worship that does not offer true honor to Jesus Christ. I cast out of myself all entities not of the Kingdom of God. I renounce all benefits from magical arts and evil in every form.

In the name of Jesus Christ I renounce any openness to the occult and separate myself from any such influences in my family life. I renounce involvement with ouija boards, horoscopes, seances, fortune telling, wearing lucky charms, and "Dungeons and Dragons." I reject movies and books on the occult. I renounce any pacts I may have made with the devil and repent of any way I sold my soul to him. Any territory handed over to the devil I now reclaim, in Jesus' name.

In the name of Jesus Christ I cast out of myself all spirits of hatred, envy, bitterness, rejection, unforgiveness, lust, gluttony, pride and sloth. I cast out spirits of lying, deceit, distortion and confusion. I renounce every spirit that would lead me astray in the correct use of the charismatic gift of the word of knowledge.

I reject all these things and ask your forgiveness, Lord Jesus, for every time I have sought knowledge apart from you. I ask your forgiveness for every time I have slipped into an occult approach to knowledge, because I wasn't centered on you. I ask your forgiveness for the ways I have not allowed you to be Lord. Cleanse and purify my heart, Lord. I receive your forgiveness, and I forgive myself.

Thank you, heavenly Father, for your eternal love. Thank you, Jesus, for giving me your Holy Spirit. Thank you, Holy Spirit, for filling me with light and love, healing, peace and joy. Amen.

Books

by
Father Robert DeGrandis, S.S.J.

The Gift of Miracles $8.00
Changed Forever $8.00
Healing Through the Mass $8.00
The Word of Knowledge $7.00
Praying for Miracles $7.00
Come Follow Me $7.00
Called to Serve $7.00
Healing the Broken Heart $6.00
Intergenerational Healing $6.00
Resting in the Spirit $6.00
Renewed by the Holy Spirit $6.00
The Gift of Prophecy $5.00
Layperson's Manual for the Healing Ministry $5.00
Growing in Jesus $5.00
To Forgive Is Divine $5.00
Coming to Life $3.00
The Power of Healing Prayer $3.00
The Gift of Tongues $3.00
Inner Healing Through the Stations of the Cross $3.00
Forgiveness and Inner Healing $3.00
Self-Image (Healing Life's Emotions) $3.00
Introduction of the Catholic Charismatic Renewal $3.00
Healing and Catholics $3.00
The Ten Commandments of Prayer $3.00
Young People's Forgiveness Prayer $2.00

Forgiveness Is Healing (The Forgiveness Prayer) $1.00
Testimony of Father Robert DeGrandis, S.S.J. $2.00
Healing the Father Relationship $2.00
Integrating Healing Into the Parish $2.00
Introduction to Inner Healing $2.00
Failure in Your Life $2.00
Receiving Holy Eucharist, the Road to Healing $2.00
Charisms $2.00
You Are the Salt of the Earth $2.00
Praising God Daily $2.00
To Love Is to Forgive $2.00
The Real Presence $3.00
Pray Your Way to Happiness $3.00

Order From Your
Local Christian Bookstore or From:
H.O.M. BOOKS
108 Aberdeen St.
Lowell, MA 01850